THE Scots MAGAZINE

LEGENDARY SCOTLAND

Myths, Folklore & Unexplained Events

△

DISCOVER THE STRANGEST TALES FROM SCOTTISH HISTORY

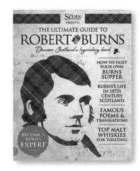

— CONTACTS —

Editorial:
2 Albert Square,
Dundee, DD1 9QJ
Tel: 01382 223131
Email: mail@scotsmagazine.com

Subscriptions:
2 Albert Square,
Dundee, DD1 9QJ
Tel: 0800 318 846
Email: shop@dctmedia.co.uk

For current subscription rates visit www.scotsmagazine.com/subscribe

For further information on The Scots Magazine's monthly magazine and branded products visit www.scotsmagazine.com

We will only use any data provided to contact people in relation to competitions or letters. You can find our privacy policy at www.dctmedia.co.uk/privacy-policy

The Scots Magazine is distributed by Frontline Ltd, Stuart House, St John's St, Peterborough, Cambridgeshire PE1 5DD.
Tel: +44 (0) 1733 555161. Website: www.frontlinedistribution.co.uk
Export Distribution (excluding AU and NZ) Seymour Distribution Ltd, 2 East Poultry Avenue, London EC1A 9PT.
Tel: +44(0)20 7429 4000 Fax: +44(0)20 7429 4001 Email: info@seymour.co.uk Website: www.seymour.co.uk

Published in Great Britain by DC Thomson & Co., Ltd., Dundee, Glasgow and London.

WELCOME

EDITOR
Katrina Patrick

DESIGN EDITOR
Nadine Stewart

PRODUCTION
Rachel McConachie

PICTURES
Ailsa Kerr

@scots_magazine
@legendaryscotland

WELCOME to *Legendary Scotland*, where you'll find some of the best monsters, ghosts and goddesses that make this wee country truly, well... legendary.

From forgotten folklore and tales of witchcraft to mythical creatures and terrifying hauntings, Scotland's past events, beliefs and traditions still shape the country today.

Every month *The Scots Magazine* team work to bring you the very best of Scotland – from dynamic cultural events to fascinating little-known sites to explore.

We love to celebrate the country's culture – a vibrant tapestry influenced by thousands of years of heritage. It weaves together threads of ancient customs with later Celtic, Gaelic and Christian beliefs to create something extraordinary.

To create *Legendary Scotland* we dug deep into our archives – all the way back to our first issue from February 1739.

Read on to discover some of the most fascinating and strangest Scottish tales we've ever published...

CONTENTS

SPIRITS

WITCHES

CREATURES

CELTIC

GHOSTS

ANCIENTS

Atmospheric Glen Coe

LAND OF LEGENDS

THE best tales get better with the telling, and that's certainly true of Scotland's legends. Scottish ghost stories and folk tales that you hear today have been honed over the generations – and centuries in some cases – since the tale's origin.

Each new telling added details and extra layers to make them more relevant to each new society that populated the land.

As new cultures and faiths tried to make sense of their surroundings – from Scotland's dramatic landscape to the stars in the sky, new theories and fables of creation emerged.

The tales surrounding the mystical standing stones of Scotland's Neolithic people is a great example of this. They were erected thousands of years ago, and

their original purpose has been lost. In tales from the later Celtic peoples, however, the stones had become the work of giants.

Then, with the arrival of St Columba and Christianity in the fifth century, these same standing stones became giants themselves, turned to stone by God for refusing to accept the new faith.

Most of Scotland's favourite stories were not written down until the 18th century or even later, previously staying alive and ever-changing purely by word of mouth.

Highland bards, or a seanchaidh as they are known in Scottish Gaelic, would tour villages and castles, telling these tall tales at both common hearthsides and royal banquets.

John Knox House and
Scottish Storytelling Centre

Celtic cross at
Iona Abbey

"The story is told eye to eye, mind to mind and heart to heart"

The Scottish Storytelling Centre on the Royal Mile in Edinburgh celebrates this oral tradition and is dedicated to keeping it alive.

"Humans are hardwired to love stories," says Daniel Abercrombie, programme and events manager, "and Scotland's greatest stories have their own home here.

"The centre is dedicated to preserving and recounting them so that future generations can enjoy these tales just as much as their forebears.

"Our ethos is nicely summed up by the old Scottish proverb, 'The story is told eye to eye, mind to mind and heart to heart.'" ○

SPIRITS

IN a land rife with superstition, every village has a tale of the supernatural to tell.

In Celtic and pagan tradition, encounters with the supernatural weren't just monster stories to frighten children, they were a part of life. All manner of beings from other worlds were believed to walk unseen beside the living.

When early Christianity was introduced to the country by Irish missionaries, like St Ninian, St Columba and St Kentigern, patron saint of Glasgow, this doctrine mingled with lingering pagan beliefs of ancient Scotland to form a fascinating fictional world of unseen spirits and demons.

Unexplained happenings are blamed on these unseen spirits, from poltergeists and wizards to the devil himself.

While ghosts are accepted as the souls of those departed, it's the spirits you need to watch out for. These beings can conjure storms, set fires and reign havoc on anyone who crosses their path. »

The mansion was
said to haunted

POLTERGEIST MANOR

A stately home in Fife was the site of numerous inexplicable events

IN the 1930s and early 1940s, incidents at a Fife mansion produced the most intensive record of poltergeist haunting in recent times.

The range of manifestations in Pitmilly House, which stood in spacious grounds near Kingsbarns, was extraordinary.

It began with all the pictures in the house being found on the floor, many of them smashed. Furniture was moved about and upset. The family lawyer was called. As he sat on an armchair in the large three-window dining room, left to reflect on the story the owner and his wife had told him, he lit a cigarette and put the burnt match in an ashtray on the arm of the chair, noting that there were seven or eight matchsticks there already.

When, later, he turned to knock off the cigarette ash the tray was empty. He found the matchsticks neatly arranged in pairs further back on the arm of the chair.

He was awakened during the night by a crash outside his bedroom and found a piece of sculpture

Below: Matchsticks were rearranged

Bottom: Furniture was moved around

The Most Haunted House In Scotland

A similar manifestation occurred in the late 1800s in Ballechin House near Ballinluig, Highland Perthshire.

The Society for Psychical Research investigated in 1897, with observers staying in the building in turns. Among the observers were the Marquis of Bute John Crichton-Stuart, soon-to-be prime minister A J Balfour, and psychical researcher Ada Goodrich Freer.

Ballechin House

"He was awakened by a crash outside his room"

on the carpet outside the door, in fragments. A few days after a sculpture bust hurtled from its pedestal in the hall and smashed against the wall, narrowly missing the head of a member of the family.

The drawing-room furnishings were found in a heap. An eight-day clock, found by a maid on three successive mornings on its face, lay smashed to splinters on the fourth.

Billiard balls disturbed the sleep of the owners by rolling about the floor in the bedroom where they had no right to be. One morning the owner's wife took the balls, one red and two **》**

Their reports were published in *The Alleged Haunting of Ballechin House* in 1899, which was serialised in *The Times*.

Reported incidents included a booming, bell-like sound that at times seemed to fill the house, associated with occasional apparitional appearances, the mysterious sound of footsteps, and the apparition of a nun.

The Society for Psychical Research later removed the reports from their proceedings on the investigation, and denounced Freer, but the house's infamy stuck.

Ballechin House was uninhabited by 1932 and finally demolished in 1963 – after a mysterious fire.

There were
unexplained fires

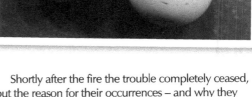

Buried billiard balls
were dug up

white, and buried them secretly in the grounds. That night they were disturbed again, and a red ball was found on the floor. She went to the spot where she had buried the balls and dug them up. The two whites were there but the red ball was gone.

Finally, one afternoon, fire broke out in a number of rooms simultaneously, originating in every case in one of the corners at the height of the ceiling.

A claim for insurance was made and met by the insurance company, who made the fullest inquiry and were satisfied that no one in the household had any responsibility for the fires.

One of the London daily newspapers, coming out with a narrative of these events, headed the article, "Scottish poltergeist makes insurance company pay up."

Shortly after the fire the trouble completely ceased, but the reason for their occurrences – and why they stopped so abruptly – is unknown to this day. **O**

"After the fire all the trouble ceased"

Words: J W HERRIES

WILL-O'-THE-WISP

Many Scots regard these mysterious lights as omens of death

TALES of mysterious lights are found in folklore throughout the world.

In Welsh tales the lights are held by little creatures called pwca, who are said to use them to lure unwitting travellers off paths and into treacherous marshlands. A similar tale is told in Southern England – there it is called the pixy-light.

In Scotland, some regard these mysterious lights as omens of death or ghosts luring travellers to their doom. Known as spunkies in Lowland Scotland, they're often blamed for shipwrecks by sailors who run aground after seeing the light on the shore and thinking it is a lighthouse.

In these parts, tales of wisps are interwoven with stories of corpse candles – phantom blue lights which linger on a funeral route. In reality, these are most likely a bioluminescent fungus.

You might have heard of wisps by their Latin name ignis fatuus, meaning "foolish fire". It's generally accepted that wisps are caused by natural gases burning above bogs or marshes – decaying organic material releases gases which can ignite when mixed with oxygen, causing a fire in mid-air.

Whether burning gas, luminous fungus or a malevolent creature – it's probably wise not to follow the wisps if you spot one on the moorland. ○

"*They lure unwitting travellers off paths and into treacherous marshlands*"

Words: KATRINA PATRICK

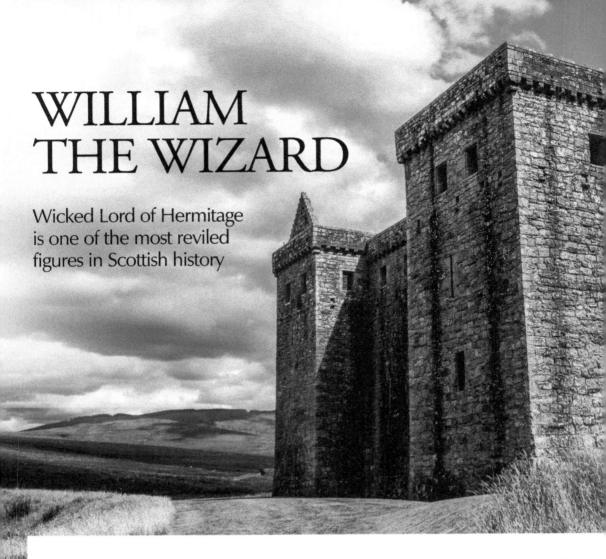

WILLIAM THE WIZARD

Wicked Lord of Hermitage is one of the most reviled figures in Scottish history

S INISTER places inspire spooky stories, and perhaps nowhere else in the country exudes brooding menace quite like Hermitage Castle in the Scottish Borders.

Local folklore tells of a demon stalking its ruins for fresh blood, a powerful wizard and of a giant whose grave lies nearby. At the centre of this web of oddities is one of the most reviled figures of Scottish history, the "Wicked" William, Lord de Soulis.

William de Soulis was Lord of Hermitage from 1318 to 1320 and allegedly spent his time terrorising the local population with killings and kidnappings.

He was said to be a wizard, though more towards the cruel, Saruman-esque side of the spectrum than the kindly Gandalf type. He was fond of the Dark Arts and subjected his people to intense cruelty with the aid of his demonic minion, Robin Redcap.

William's reputation was so foul that a marauding Northumbrian giant, known as the Cout of Kielder, who came to slay him was seen as a hero – not a title giants are generally accustomed to.

Alas, the giant was lured by William's sorcery into an eddy in the nearby burn and drowned.

Finally, the locals revolted against their wizard

Main: Hermitage Castle

Below: Sir Walter Scott

Bottom: The ballad telling William's story

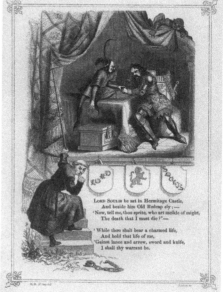

"He subjected his people to intense cruelty"

laird. They found he was invulnerable when pitted against common weaponry, but a popular 18th-century Border ballad recounted by Sir Walter Scott tells of how they bound him with lead and boiled him alive in a brass cauldron upon the nearby stone circle – the Ninestane Rig – thus finally ending his hold over the land. ○

Words: DAVID WEINCZOK

Legendary Scotland   17

THE WOLF OF BADENOCH

Scots king's vicious son burned Elgin Cathedral to the ground

SCOTTISH history is littered with villains, but there can be few as vile and vicious as Alexander Stewart. Known as the Wolf of Badenoch, he raped and pillaged, murdering and marauding across the north and north-east of Scotland in the latter part of the 14th century.

It seems that the sobriquet of "the Wolf" was only bestowed after his death – perhaps confirming the fear he engendered across the entire country – but another effective moniker attached to Stewart was the "Celtic Attila".

Born in 1343, he was the fourth son of King Robert II of Scotland. He used his power to rampage across the

Highlands, fathering around 40 illegitimate children, and burning Elgin Cathedral to the ground in a temper tantrum after being excommunicated by the Bishop of Moray.

The strangest part of his story, however, was the manner of his death. The Wolf of Badenoch reportedly died in 1394 after playing chess with the devil at Ruthven Castle, near Aviemore.

It is said that after the church excommunicated Alexander, the devil came to call. A tall man dressed in black knocked on the castle door in the middle of the night and challenged the Wolf to a game of chess.

Alexander agreed, and the pair set up a table in the

The site of Ruthven Castle, now Ruthven Barracks

Pictures: ASHLEIGH MACKENZIE Words: KATRINA PATRICK

The burning of Elgin Cathedral

Statue of Alexander Stewart

"The devil challenged the Wolf to a game of chess"

banqueting hall and played through the night. It is said a terribly storm began to form around the castle as the pair played on.

In the morning, the Wolf's servants were all found outside the castle walls, apparently struck dead by lightning.

The Wolf himself was found lifeless in the banqueting hall. There was not a mark on him but, strangely, the nails in his boots were torn from the leather. ○

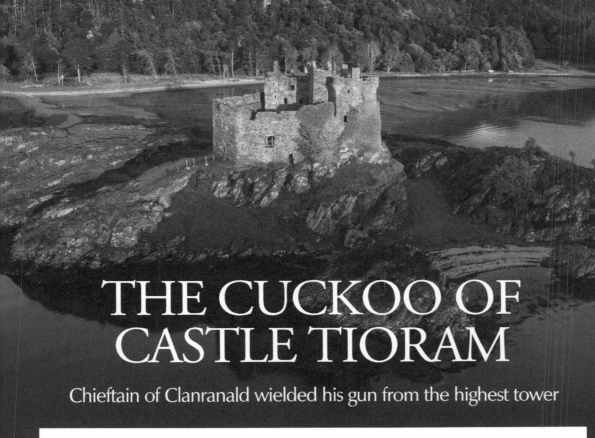

THE CUCKOO OF CASTLE TIORAM

Chieftain of Clanranald wielded his gun from the highest tower

DONALD, the 13th chieftain of Clanranald, ruled Castle Tioram on Loch Moidart, Lochaber, in the 17th century – and was known as a madman.

The story goes that Donald would stand atop the highest tower cradling his gun – dubbed The Cuckoo – and shoot anyone who came near.

His dastardly deeds included killing a kinsman who had come to visit him, breaching sacred laws of guest right, and marooning a servant to be drowned.

It seems Donald's deeds reached the ear of the devil, for a familiar spirit in the form of a giant black frog began following him wherever he went.

Terrified, he left it in a corner of the castle and sailed for Lochboisdale, South Uist, only to find it waiting for him on the shore when he arrived.

He locked it in a dungeon and made for Arisaig – but the frog appeared swimming beside his ship.

When Donald died on Canna in 1686, the frog vanished and a great crack – like the sound of The Cuckoo firing – was heard.

Strangely, many historical records skip a generation of the Clanranald chieftains, hopping straight from the 12th chieftain John, to whom these deeds are often attributed, to the 14th chieftain Allan Dearg – missing out the dreaded Donald altogether.

Which is a worse fate – being remembered as a tyrant or not being remembered at all? ○

"A giant black frog began following him"

Words: DAVID WEINCZOK

THE HAUNTING OF RINGCROFT

The chilling tale of a poltergeist who terrorised a Galloway family

T HE Ringcroft case in Galloway is one of the earliest and most carefully detailed accounts of poltergeist manifestations.

In 1695, the Rev Alexander Telfair, minister of the parish of Rerrick in the Stewartry of Kirkcudbright, recorded his experiences. He wrote of the "apparition, expressions and actings of a spirit" that infested the house of Andrew Mackie, Ringcroft of Stocking, in the parish of Rerrick.

Andrew Mackie's troubles apparently began in February 1695, when he discovered that the bindings which secured his beasts had been loosened and broken overnight. Blaming the animals, he made stronger bindings, but they, too, were broken mysteriously.

He then moved his beasts to another outbuilding, and the first night thereafter found one of the animals bound with a "hair-tedder" to the back of the house in such a way that the feet of the poor animal scarcely touched the ground.

Shortly afterwards, when the family was asleep one night, a creel of peats were placed together in the middle of the floor by unseen hands and then set alight. >>

Peat was set alight

A white hand was visible

Fortunately, the smoke wakened Mackie and his family, otherwise both house and occupants would have been destroyed.

As time passed, the "manifestations" increased in frequency and severity. In March of that year stones were being hurled all over the interior of the house, – for four days and nights, witnessed by many people.

The matter was reported by Mackie to Telfair, the minister of the parish, who visited the house a day or two later. At first nothing happened and the minister was standing at the barn end, about to take his departure, when he saw two stones drop on the house.

Immediately, those inside the house began to cry out that the spirit was at it again. Telfair then went into the house and, as he prayed, several stones were thrown at him from unseen hands.

Later in the week, Telfair spent a night at the house and was greatly troubled. Stones and several other objects were thrown at him, and he was struck several times on the sides and shoulders very sharply with a great staff – with those who were present hearing the noise of the strokes. There was rapping on chests and boards, as if someone was calling for access.

That night, as Rev Telfair was at prayer, he felt something pressing on his arm and saw a little white hand and arm from the elbow down.

After that the spirit became more active and more abusive than ever – not only to the Mackie family, but also to neighbours who came to visit them.

Some were dragged up and down the house by their clothes. The local miller from Auchencairn, Keige by name, was gripped so forcibly that he called to his neighbours for help. At other times the door bar and other furnishings would move through the house as if being carried. Yet no person could be seen.

Main: The events took place near Kirkcudbright

Below: The local minster was called to help

"He felt something pressing on his arm and saw a little white hand and arm"

Finally, Charles Macklelland of Colline, the landlord, and Mackie attended a meeting of ministers at nearby Buittle and gave them an account of the matter.

Two of the ministers, Andrew Ewart of Kells and John Murdo of Crossmichael, visited the house and spent a night there, fasting and praying. They, too, had a rough time. Great stones, some of them seven pounds in weight, were thrown at them.

Stones were thrown

No one in the house that night escaped from the spirit's fury and cruelty. Fiery peats were thrown at people and at dawn, when they rose from prayer, stones poured down on all who were in the house.

And so it went on. William Macminn, a blacksmith, was wounded on the head by a flying stone. A plough sock was cast at him, followed by a stone trough which landed on his back – though, remarkably, he was unhurt. Twice the house was set on fire, but luckily no serious damage was done.

As the local ministers were at that time meeting at Kirkcudbright, five of their number were appointed to go to the house with Telfair – to spend as much time as possible in fasting and prayer.

"No sooner did I begin to open my mouth," records Telfair, "than it threw stones at me and all within the house.

"It came often with such force upon the house that it made all the walls to shake, it broke a hole through the timber and thatch of the house and poured in great »

Ministers prayed at the house

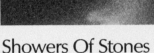

Stone-throwing is a common feature

"Fiery peats were thrown at people"

stones, one whereof, more than a quarter weight, fell upon Mr Monteith's back – Rev John Monteith, minister of Borgue – yet he was not hurt. It threw another with great force at him when he was praying, yet he was neither hurt nor moved thereby."

Once, a voice was heard warning all within hearing that it had been sent to warn the land to repent, and if the land did not repent it would go to its father and get a commission to return with a hundred worse than itself – and would trouble every family in the land.

After many more acts of violence and fire-raising, mingled with spoken threats, the manifestations suddenly ceased. Alexander Telfair concluded his remarkable narration with the following words, "Now all things aforesaid being of undoubted verity, therefore I conclude with that of the Apostle, 1. Peter v., 8-9 – Be sober, be vigilant, because your adversary the devil,

Showers Of Stones

The throwing of stones, as in the Ringcroft case is a theme reported at supposed poltergeist hauntings around the world.

Lithobolia: or, the Stone-Throwing Devil is a 7000-word narrative folk tale by Richard Chamberlayne, first printed in 1698.

It records the apparently true events of New Castle in the US where hundreds of stones mysteriously rained down on George Walton's tavern over the entire summer of 1682.

There have been various reports of stone-throwing poltergeists across the centuries, but the most recent to have made headlines was in Birmigham in 1981, when even a police inquiry could not identify the source of stones being thrown at residents of Thornton Road.

as a roaring lion, walketh about seeking whom he devour. Whom resist steadfast in the faith."

The location of the Ringcroft cottage, which has long since vanished, was marked by a row of four trees conspicuous on the skyline near Auchencairn.

Of the four, one remains – a single, dead tree guarding the site of the cottage, the foundations of which are still there. O

Words: CB PHIN

DEVILS IN DISGUISE

There are many tall tales of the devil and his followers in Scotland

1 Nicknames

The devil wears many guises in Scottish folklore and has many names. The National Bard, Robert Burns, recorded many of these names in his poems of the 18th century, referring to the devil as Auld Hornie, Malhoun, Auld Hangie, the Deil, and sometimes Clootie – he of the cloven hoof.

2 The Devil's Pulpit

In Finnich Gorge, Stirlingshire, you'll find a mushroom-shaped rock that rises up from the blood-red waters of the Carnock Burn. It is said this is where the devil stood to address his followers. Thankfully, the burn's red tinge comes from the sandstone the water flows over and not from anything more sinister.

3 Slaugh

This is the name given to a group of very dangerous spirits from the Highlands and Western Isles. They are known as the unforgiven dead in Gaelic folklore, and raised by the devil. The slaugh are usually malevolent, although there are tales of them rescuing people from cliffs. Sometimes thought to be fallen angels or souls of the dead, the slaugh fly through the air at Hallowe'en.

4 Black Donald

In the Highlands the devil is known as Black Donald, or Black Duncan, and his defining characteristic is his cloven hooves which give away his varied disguises. John Gregorson Campbell's *The Gaelic Otherworld*, first published in 1900, gives a detailed account of several sightings of Black Donald, his physical appearance, and his dark deeds when summoned by magicians.

5 The Devil's Beeftub

A few miles north of Moffat in the Scottish Borders, a hidden hollow that nestles between four hills is known locally as the Devil's Beeftub. During the Reiver period, from around 1300 to

1610, many clans of the Borders would steal cattle from the English Reivers over the border and hide them in this hollow. The protection it gave the stolen cattle was seen as the work of the devil, hence the enduring nickname.

Words: KATRINA PATRICK

WITCHES
△

DESPITE being such a small country, Scotland was one of Europe's most notorious persecutors of witches during the 16th and 17th centuries. It's estimated that 4000 people, mainly women, were put to death during this time – double the number that faced the same fate in England.

Although the witches were predominately female, around 15% of the accused were men. People were accused of witchcraft for many reasons from demonic possession and maleficium to folk healing. Superstition was rife and people would often believe any misfortune in their lives was the result of a spell being cast on them.

Accusations would often occur after a quarrel between friends or neighbours. Large groups of women would be accused, with people interpreting their close friendship as proof that they were part of a coven.

Once a witch had been accused, evidence would be gathered for a trial. This usually involved the alleged witch being tortured, often in the form of sleep deprivation, which would cause them to hallucinate and even confess to the alleged crime.

Discover some of Scotland's most notorious witch trials on the following pages, and the fates that befell the ordinary men and women who stood accused. »

Beatrix was held in the Tolbooth

Pittenweem beach

PITTENWEEM TRIALS

Villagers imprisoned, tortured and killed over a teenager's accusation

IN 1704 in Pittenweem, Fife, a 16-year-old apprentice blacksmith, Patrick Morton, was asked by his neighbour Beatrix Laing, to make some nails.

When Patrick cheekily replied that he was too busy, Beatrix walked off in a huff, furiously muttering something under her breath – presumably along the lines of "kids these days."

When Patrick became ill just a few days later, however, he suspected that Beatrix's mutterings were in fact a curse.

As his illness progressed he became convinced that she had cast a spell and was sending evil thoughts to torture him. He confided his worries to local minister Patrick Cowper, who persuaded the boy to report Beatrix to the authorities.

The minister, who must have been one nasty piece of work, also managed to convince the lad to accuse several other villagers along with Beatrix. No one thought to investigate the reasoning behind the boy's accusations and the suspected witches were imprisoned in Pittenweem Tolbooth.

Beatrix was confined to a dark cell for five months while subjected to horrific torture. On being released with a fine, she was chased out of town by the locals.

She found safety in nearby St Andrews, but she died alone shortly after her arrival.

"An angry mob dragged her to the beach"

Another of the accused, the elderly Thomas Brown starved to death in his cell. The Pittenweem witch case was eventually dismissed by the Privy Council in Edinburgh, but when one of the accused, Janet Cornfoot, escaped from prison, an angry mob seized her and dragged her down to Pittenweem Beach.

Janet was pelted with stones, then covered by a door, which was weighed down by heavy boulders.

Peine forte et dure

This method of torture, known as *peine forte et dure*, was also used to execute accused Giles Corey at the Salem Witch Trials 11 years before.

When Janet had died, a horse and cart was driven over her repeatedly to make sure the devil's soul was squashed out of her and wouldn't return. Refused a Christian burial, her body was thrown into a communal grave with that of Thomas Brown at the spot in Pittenweem known as Witch Corner.

It was intended that when the rest of the accused were found guilty and burned at the stake, the bodies would be exhumed and thrown to the flames.

Thomas Brown's family and friends smuggled his body out of Witch Corner and reburied it in consecrated grounds. All the other accused were eventually freed, however, and the apprentice blacksmith Patrick Morton was later exposed as a liar.

Despite this, neither he nor the mob that killed Janet Cornfoot were ever brought to justice. O

Words: DAWN GEDDES

THE QUEEN OF
SCOTTISH WITCHES

Confessions of flying, making potions and meeting with the devil

ISOBEL GOWDIE, a young housewife from Auldearn, Nairnshire, was one of Scotland's most infamous witches. While most of the evidence presented can now be easily dismissed as nonsense, Isobel's admissions during her trial in 1662 started the myths that still surround witches today.

Isobel and her husband led an unremarkable life in the area around Loch Loy, just north of Auldearn. Isobel was illiterate, and spent her days doing basic household chores and tasks such as milking, making bread, and weaving.

It is unclear how Isobel first came to trial, but it is thought that the local minister Harry Forbes, a zealous extremist who feared witches, accused her of conspiring against him.

After being accused of witchcraft, Isobel spectacularly confessed to a number of abhorrent acts.

The investigators found the Devil's Mark on her shoulder, and Isobel agreed saying she had been baptised by the devil, who laid his mark on her. Isobel described the devil as a "meikle black roch man" with forked and cloven feet.

Isobel said she met the devil

Auldearn countryside

"Isobel said she'd been baptised by the devil"

In four separate confessions given over a six-week period, no doubt while being held and interrogated in dreadful conditions, Isobel confessed to 15 years' involvement with the devil, who gave her a new name – Janet.

Isobel also claimed to be able to fly to her coven meetings, a group of 13 – a number which became absorbed into standard depiction of witchcraft. She claimed they made a potion with the body of an unchristened child to take away the fruit of a local farmer's corn.

Isobel said she was regularly entertained by the King and Queen of the Fairies in the land of the elves under the hills. **»**

The Devil's Mark

Searching for the Devil's Mark – also known as the Witches' Mark – was one of the many ways witch-hunters convinced themselves, and the jury, that they had found their prey. Those accused of witchcraft had their bodies scrutinised for such marks, which would then be pricked to test if they were sensitive. If no pain was felt or the wound did not bleed, their abusers took it to mean they had caught a witch.

Searching for the Devil's Mark

To add to the humiliation, this was usually carried out in front of a crowd of braying onlookers, and the women were often shaved from head to toe. Eyelids, armpits and private places were inspected, and if the alleged witch happened to have no blemishes, the accusers were undeterred. They simply said that the devil had left an invisible mark, and so they pricked her all over with a pin until they found a tough area of skin that didn't bleed. Some believed that the devil created each mark with his claws or a hot iron. Others thought he licked his followers, and the contact would leave a mysterious blemish. Except, of course, these were not mysterious blemishes but moles, skin tags, birthmarks or scars – but to the hunters, they were irrefutable proof they had caught a witch.

Left: Her tales became a standard depiction of witchcraft

Below: Isobel was likely burned at the stake

The transcripts of her confessions feature many inclusions of "et cetera" which cut short her lengthy monologues of fantasy, suggesting even the witchfinders were unsure of her stories.

The source of Isobel's tales have been debated over the years. Many believe Isobel was mentally ill, while others speculate that she created the tales based on folklore of the time as a way of avoiding further questioning.

On April 10, 1662, the Privy Council in Edinburgh issued a proclamation prohibiting torture being used as a means of securing confessions from witches – unless it was specifically authorised by the Council.

Although probably imprisoned for the six-week duration of her confessions, it would appear that Isobel spoke freely without being under duress.

The Council advised she should be found guilty

"Isobel's confessions started a new wave of persecutions"

only if the confessions had been volunteered without torture, that they were sane and without a wish to die.

Whatever the real story, Isobel's confessions earned her the nickname the Queen of Scottish Witches, and although subsequent records have been lost, it is presumed that she was burned at the stake shortly after her trial.

Many Christian authorities considered witchcraft a post-Christian Satanic cult – rather than the surviving religion of pre-Christian Europe – and Isobel's confessions about the devil helped them start a new wave of persecutions in Scotland during the reign of Charles II.

Many characteristics we associate with witches today come from Isobel's detailed, spectacular and inexplicable confessions. O

Words: DAWN GEDDES

GRISSELL JAFFRAY

The last alleged witch to be burned at the stake in Dundee

"All three of the accusers were leading ministers"

A MARRIED healer and fortune teller, or "spaewife" as they were known in Scotland, Grissell Jaffray was the last victim of witchhunts in Dundee.

Grissell was the final alleged witch to be burned at the stake in the city in 1669. The details of Grissell's case are unrecorded, but we do know she stood accused of "the horrid crime of witchcraft" alongside her husband James Butchart, a burgess of Dundee and upstanding member of the community.

All three of the accusers were leading ministers in the Dundee presbytery at the time – Harry Scrymsour of St Mary's, John Guthrie of South Church and William Rait of Third Charge, now St Paul's.

At the Jaffray witch trial only Grissell was found guilty, however, and she was sentenced to death by strangulation before her body was burned at the stake.

Memorial mosaic

Legend has it that Grissell's son returned to Dundee by boat to fight against his mother's execution. On his arrival he saw the smoke rising from the city and realised that he was too late to save her.

Devastated, the sailor turned his ship around without making port and never returned to the city.

Although not found guilty, the fate of Grissell's husband James wasn't a pleasant one either, though nothing compared to poor Grissell. He lost his title, wealth and standing, and died in a poorhouse several years later.

The story of Grissell's life captivated imaginations and has been fictionalised for the novels *Witches Blood* by William Blain and *The Curewife* by Claire-Marie Watson.

In Dundee, there is a mosaic memorial to Grissell Jaffray on the cobblestones of Peter Street and a plaque marking the spot where she died. O

Words: DAWN GEDDES

ROYAL REVENGE

James VI started a Scottish witch hunt with the North Berwick trials

MAY DAY eve is Walpurgis Night, the date when witches are said to fly on broomsticks to the peaks of the Harz Mountains in Germany to celebrate the arrival of spring.

In Scotland, the supernatural was seen as just another part of life, but witches were a phenomenon only peasants believed in. There was a shift in perception, however, after a collection of German superstitions were published, named *Malleus*

Maleficarum. The popular book and its ideas filtered through Europe, influencing the public and the church.

People started to become wary of witches, believing that they might put their powers to devilish use. This fear grew and witchcraft was officially outlawed in Scotland in 1563. Thousands of horrific trials took place between the 16th and 18th centuries, as neighbour turned on neighbour and accusations flew.

It might be more than 300 years since the last person

Witches are believed to fly to the Harz mountains on Walpurgis night

accused of being a witch in Scotland was executed, but the macabre period has not been forgotten.

The first major witch trial in Scotland took place at North Berwick in 1591. The trial lasted two years and once Geillis Duncan was burned at the stake the country became obsessed.

Geillis worked as a maid for the local deputy bailiff, David Seaton, in Tranent near North Berwick. When Geillis started to sneak out at night, David became suspicious. When she suddenly seemed to have the power to heal the injured and cure the ill, he accused her of being a witch, and demanded that she explain her strange behaviour and new-found skills.

When no explanation was forthcoming, he had the poor maid tortured.

Geillis refused to admit to her alleged crimes, but her tormentors – who used despicable devices such as pilliwinks, or thumbscrews, to force a confession – found what they said was the Devil's Mark on her neck.

She was immediately thrown into prison. News reached King James VI that a witch had been caught in the area. He and his wife Anne has just been caught in a fierce storm in the North Sea, and the royal couple immediately accused Scotland's witches of summoning the storms to destroy their ship.

James launched a witch hunt, inspired by those »

"The royal couple accused Scotland's witches of summoning storms to destroy their ship"

Storms were blamed on Scottish witches

James VI

Words: DAWN GEDDES

he'd heard about in Norway and Denmark, and arrived to interrogate Geillis himself. She revealed the names of several other people she claimed had been practising the dark arts alongside her.

Geillis spoke of having been on a boat named the *Grace of God* with the Devil and other members of the alleged coven, where merrymaking and mayhem ensued. She also admitted to casting a spell on a hat belonging to the laird of Balnaird. After months of torture, she was sentenced to death.

On December 4, 1591, the day of her execution, she was taken to Castle Hill in Edinburgh. In a final statement, she announced that everything she'd said about her co-accused was untrue, and that she'd made it all up because the horrors inflicted on her by David Seaton had been too much to bear.

Sadly, it was too late for two of her co-accused,

> ## "The alleged witches were left with no choice but to confess"

Mary, Queen of Scots

Euphame and Barbara, as both are thought to have already been executed, and it was too late for Geillis herself. Historians widely believe that the torture of Geillis and the other alleged witches was so brutal, they would have been left with little choice but to confess.

The North Berwick Witch Trials continued for two years, and more than 70 people were investigated.

This was far from the end of James's crackdown, however. In 1597, he published *Daemonologie* – or to use its longer title, *Daemonologie, In Forme of a Dialogue, Divided into Three Books: By the High and Mighty Prince, James &c.*

It was split into three sections: magic and necromancy; witchcraft and sorcery; and spirits and spectres. It wasn't a handbook, of course. James didn't want to help budding witches and wizards learn their craft – instead, he wanted to drum up as much fear as possible.

It's thought that his unhealthy obsession with the occult was triggered by the violent death of his mother, Mary, Queen of Scots, who was beheaded. He saw the book not only as a warning to the people of Scotland, but a call to arms for witch-hunters. His mission was successful in the country – convictions of witchcraft increased exponentially.

When he became King of England, however, as James I, he was disappointed to discover that witch-hunts and executions were on the decline

Daemonologie

there – in fact, the English had started to doubt witches existed at all. He had *Daemonologie* reprinted twice in the first year of his reign, and decided to revise English law while he was at it.

The Witchcraft Act of 1604 took a zero tolerance approach to the dark arts, making hanging the punishment for even first-time offenders.

This was eventually replaced with the Witchcraft act of 1735, which seemed to acknowledged that witchcraft wasn't real – it only enforced penalties on those was claimed the "pretence of witchcraft".

Strangely, however, the Witchcraft Act of 1735 remained in force in Britain well into the 20th century, until its eventual repeal with the enactment of the Fraudulent Mediums Act of 1951. ○

North Berwick

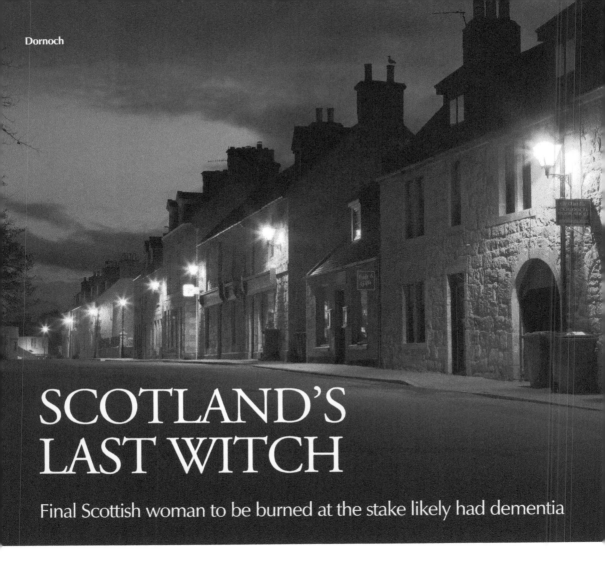

SCOTLAND'S LAST WITCH

Final Scottish woman to be burned at the stake likely had dementia

JANET HORNE lived in Dornoch with her daughter, who was born with a disability affecting the shape of her hands and feet.

Her neighbours gossiped about the lone elderly woman, speculating that her daughter's feet looked just like hoofs.

They accused poor Janet of turning the young woman into a pony so that she could ride her through the countryside carrying out the work of the devil.

Janet and her daughter were swiftly arrested and tried for the crime of witchcraft.

Captain David Ross, sheriff-depute of Sutherland, quickly found both women guilty, and sentenced them to death by burning the next day.

Fortunately, the younger woman managed to escape, but poor Janet was tarred and feathered then paraded through the streets of Dornoch to her execution.

The elderly woman, who is now thought to have been suffering from dementia, warmed her hands by the very flames that were waiting to consume her. She smiled and called them "a bonny blaze".

Stone marking the site where Janet died

The accused warmed her hands at the fire

Janet was tarred and feathered

Words: DAWN GEDDES

"Suspicion, speculation and gossip can easily escalate into fear and terror"

This was 1727, and the methods that had been used to confirm the guilt of thousands of witches began to be scrutinised and rejected. Janet was the last to be executed for the crime of witchcraft, and the law was eventually completely abolished in 1736.

In Dornoch today there is a stone marker, erected in the 1900s, in the spot where Janet met her end.

Although the days of burning accused witches at the stake are thankfully long over, it's important that we never let the mistakes of our past slip far from our minds.

The Scottish witch trials may just be one chilling chapter in our country's great history, but while we continue to live in a world where suspicion, speculation and gossip can easily escalate into fear and terror, the mistakes of our past will never truly leave us.

The crime of witchcraft was abolished in 1736. ○

THE WITCHES' WELL

Edinburgh memorial to the thousands killed in Scotland's witch trials

T HE Witches' Well is one of Edinburgh's many fascinating curiosities, and honours those who suffered during a dark period in Scotland's past.

This old drinking fountain commemorates the thousands of Scots who were accused of witchcraft between the 15th and 18th centuries. Many were put to death on Castlehill, where the Witches' Well can be found – if you know where to look.

A plaque above the fountain explains the design, "the wicked head and serene head signify that some used their exceptional knowledge for evil purposes while others were misunderstood and wished their kind nothing but good."

There's also an evil eye on one side of the trough and a pair of healing hands on the other.

Water from the city's reservoir – now the Tartan Weaving Mill, which is where you'll spot this fountain-turned-planter – would have been pumped through the hole beneath the suitably sinister snake's head.

Most visitors to the nearby castle don't know it's there, but this pretty, poignant little piece of history is definitely worth seeking out. O

The Witches' Well today

Find the well on Castlehill

Words: LAURA BROWN

OCCULT SECRETS

Mystical potions, spells, prophecies and the supernatural

1 Origins

The first recorded evidence of witches comes from the Bible. *The Book of Samuel,* in *The Old Testament,* thought to be written between 630 and 540 BCE, tells of the Witch of Endor. King Saul was battling the Philistine army, and he asked the Witch of Endor to summon the dead prophet Samuel's spirit to help him.

2 Weird Sisters

The three witches in William Shakespeare's *Macbeth* are based on Holinshed's 1587 *Chronicles of England, Scotland, and Ireland,* in which three "Weird Sisters" prophesise that King Macbeth "should neuer be slaine with man borne of anie woman, nor vanquished till the wood of Bernane came to the castell of Dunsinane."

3 War Witch

During the Second World War, Helen Duncan, from Callander, claimed a dead sailor told her the *HMS Barham* had been sunk. This information had not been released to the public and Duncan was arrested under the Witchcraft Act 1735. After a seven-day trial, she was sentenced to nine months in London's Holloway Prison.

4 Guilty!

A study by the University of Edinburgh into the history of witchcraft in Scotland found that 32% of all accusations took place in the Lothians around Edinburgh. The study also found that of all those accused across Scotland, 67% were found guilty, compared to only 25% in England – such was the hysteria at the time.

5 Hereditary Healers

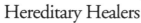

The Beaton clan were a medical dynasty in Scotland between the 15th and 17th centuries. Known for their healing prowess, the family provided medical services to the Royal House of Scotland using traditional and herbal methods.

Members of the clan gradually gave up their trade, however, with the rise of witch trials. In 1567, Janet Beaton, an attendant of Mary, Queen of Scots, was accused with her niece Mary Beaton of using witchcraft to cause the queen to fall in love with Lord Darnley. O

Words: KATRINA PATRICK

CREATURES

THE Loch Ness Monster, a dinosaur-like creature that is said to live in the murky depths of Loch Ness, is famous around the world – but she's far from the only Scottish mythical creature.

If you believe the stories, our lochs, forests and mountains are teeming with strange and wonderful beings – both evil and benign.

Some have a never-ending thirst for human blood, a few lie in wait to lure weary travellers off country paths to their doom, some are merely curious about humans, while others are just happy to help with the housework.

These beasties are a popular and enduring part of Scottish folklore, so much so that even the country's official national animal is a mythical creature, the unicorn.

A symbol of purity and power in Celtic mythology, the unicorn featured on William I's royal coat of arms in the 12th century and is still used on Queen Elizabeth's today. »

THE FAIRY KINGDOM

Keep on the right side of these creatures to avoid their vengeance

Fairies or faeries, as they are often known, are an important part of Scottish folklore. These creatures are said to be able to change their shape and size, although many appear in tiny human form.

While most of us think of fairies as being joyful creatures, according to legend they can be rather devious and enjoy playing tricks on humans. The female of the species, although beautiful, is known to be particularly malevolent.

Fairies prefer to avoid humans if possible, choosing to dwell in remote hills, mountains and near water pools instead. When humans enter their territory, we should treat their domain with respect, and avoid wearing green – the colour of the fairies.

When discussing fairies, we should choose our words carefully – for even if we can't see them, it doesn't mean that they can't see us.

Highlanders would often refer to fairies as "good people", even when they believed they were up to no good. The terms, "the good neighbours", "the

A green path leads to fairyland

"They are devious and enjoy playing tricks"

Illustration of Thomas Rhymer's ballad

Changelings

According to the legend, when a fairy steals a child, it leaves a changeling in its place. The changeling may look identical to the stolen baby, but displays characteristics that alert its parents to the fact that their child has been replaced.

These can include a change in behaviour, such as being grouchy or crying a lot, a change in colour, failure to thrive or not growing as it should.

Of course, these days we would recognise these as signs of illness, but in the 18th century, when superstition was rife, parents would truly believe that their child had been taken.

A changeling

In a bid to get their baby back, anguished parents would leave the changeling out on a fairy hill at midnight in the hope that the fairy folk would see one of their own in peril and take in back into the fold, returning the stolen baby.

If the baby was alive in the morning it would mean the fairies had returned it, but if it wasn't the parents would believe their child was playing eternally in the fairy realm.

fairfolk" and "the people of the peace", were also common throughout Scotland.

In the 13th century, Scots poet and laird, Thomas of Erceldoune, became famous for his inability to lie, and for several prophecies which came true. When asked how he came by these gifts, Thomas wrote his famous ballad, *Thomas Rhymer and the Queen of Elfland*, which recounts his own encounter with a fairy.

In the song, Thomas speaks of meeting a fairy queen who was dressed in green and riding a horse with silver bells in its mane. In the poem, the fairy queen forbids Thomas from eating anything **»**

Fairies live in remote places such as the Fairy Pools on Skye

"The queen takes him back to her fairy kingdom"

James VI

other than what she brings him – and he obeys. She then shows him three paths, one with thorns that leads to heaven, one fair and lovely that leads to hell, and lastly a green path that leads to fairyland.

She leads him down the green path and tells him, "ye maun hold your tongue, Whatever ye may hear or see, For, if you speak a word in Elflyn land, Ye'll neer get back to your ain countrie." The queen then takes him back to her fairy kingdom for seven years.

Once his seven years were up, he returned home with the gift of prophecy. Thomas went on to make several accurate prophecies – notably the death of Alexander III, and James VI inheriting the throne of England. ○

Words: DAWN GEDDES

THE DRAGON OF DUNDEE

Lovestruck neighbour defeats beast that killed nine daughters

ONCE upon a time, in the village of Pitempton, just outside Dundee, a farmer lived with his nine daughters.

One day, he sent his youngest daughter to the well to bring back water for the family. But she never returned.

He despatched another daughter to look for her. She didn't come back either. So he sent another, then another, then another, until all nine of his daughters had gone to the well. None of them made it home.

He went to search for them, but was met by a tragic scene. His daughters had been killed by a fearsome dragon.

The farmer ran to tell his neighbours what had happened, and they vowed to slay the dragon together.

A brave man named Martin, in love with the farmer's eldest daughter, was the one who finally managed to

The sculpture in Dundee

kill the formidable beast, encouraged by his band of neighbours shouting "Strike, Martin!".

The area soon became known as Strikemartin, later morphing into Strathmartine. Martin's Stone marks the spot where the dragon died.

A statue of the dragon, sculpted by Tony Morrow, now sits in Dundee's Murraygate. O

A dragon is said to have killed the girls

Martin's Stone

THE GREY MAN OF BEN MACDUI

Scotland's very own yeti lurks around the Lairg Ghru pass

THE mountains of Tibet, the USA's Pacific North-West, the dense jungles of Sumatra – these are all places where, according to legend, an unlucky traveller might come across one of folklore's most fascinating creatures.

Bigfoot, Yeti, Orang Pendek, Yowie – people all over the world have given these creatures many names, but did you know that Scotland has its very own?

Am Fear Liath Mor, or The Big Grey Man of Ben Macdui, is no ordinary beast. It all started in 1891, when John Norman Collie, the famous mountaineer, scientist and explorer, believed he saw something strange lurking in the wilds near Ben Macdui, the highest mountain in the Cairngorm National Park.

Collie kept what he'd seen to himself for 35 years, before speaking of his encounter at the 1925 meeting of the Cairngorm Society. Collie was by the summit, on a misty day, when he heard footsteps.

"As if someone was walking after me but taking steps three or four times the length of my own," he said.

Collie could see nothing, but the eerie crunching sound continued. Finally, he was overcome with panic and terror and rushed down the mountainside, running until he dared stop. "Whatever you make of it I do not know," Collie told the meeting. "But there is something very queer about the top of Ben Macdui and I will not go back there myself."

"There is something very queer about the top of Ben Macdui"

Slopes of Ben Macdui

Word of Collie's encounter spread and, before long, he started receiving letters from other people who said that they too had seen something strange there – most often below the skyline near the Lairg Ghru pass.

Dr A.M. Kellas and his brother, Henry, spoke of a giant figure approaching them near the summit. Author, Richard Frere, told a story about a friend who'd seen a giant figure walking down the mountainside. Mountaineer, Alexander Tewnion, claimed to have actually shot a creature on Ben Macdui – 3m (10ft) tall, broad shouldered and covered in short hair, brown or olive, walking upright, with long arms. The descriptions seem to match other wildman sightings.

Mostly, however, the creature is not seen – people simply sense the presence of something threatening and malevolent and, overcome by uncontrollable fear, panic and despondency, they bolt down the mountainside to safety. Some report ghostly voices, and there are many »

Norman Collie, left

Illustration of a yeti

James Hogg

" Hogg was amazed when the figure started mimicking his movements "

accounts of ghostly footsteps and even eerie music. Others talk of being drawn, hypnotically, to the edge of dangerous ravines.

As to what, if anything, the Big Grey Man might be, opinions are divided.

An unknown creature that emits pheromones or low-frequency sounds that disorientate humans?

Similar feelings of despondency and panic have been in reports of sasquatch sightings in Canada. Or, could an ancient or even prehistoric species of ape or human be living in the Cairngorms? One interesting suggestion is

that these creatures pass through an inter-dimensional portal, somewhere on the mountain, which apparently explains the shimmering and the fact that people hear but don't see them.

There are more rational explanations, however. In 1791, poet and shepherd James Hogg was terrified when he saw a huge ghostly figure while out near Ben Macdui tending his sheep.

Hogg was doubly amazed when the figure started mimicking his movements. A wildman with a sense of humour, or an example of Brocken spectre? This

A Brocken spectre

scientific phenomena takes its name from the Brocken peak in the Harz Mountains, Germany. This optical illusion is seen when the observer's apparently huge, magnified shadow is cast onto the mist or clouds by sunlight.

The observer over-estimates the size of the shadow because they compare it to faraway objects seen through gaps in the mist or clouds. Sometimes, when the cloud moves, the shadow appears to move with them.

Fortean investigator, Andy Roberts, believes the Big Grey Man sightings are symptoms of what he calls mountain panic – that is, fear and anxiety brought on by isolation and exhaustion.

Roberts spoke to mountaineers who'd experienced uncontrollable fits of panic while climbing elsewhere in Scotland, in Wales and in Papua New Guinea.

Roberts puts the appearance of the strange creatures down to folk tales about giants and other ghoulish creatures said to inhabit the Cairngorms. Jury's out, though – what's your verdict? O

FALLEN ANGELS

The selkie seal folk can walk on land and look human

SEALS or seal folk, have always played an important role in Scottish mythology, with the sea creatures often being viewed as fallen angels, too good to send to hell.

Originating from the folklore of Orkney and Shetland, a selkie or silkie, is a special species of seal which holds the ability to disguise itself in human form. This magical gift allows a selkie to remove their seal skins and walk among mortal beings, undiscovered.

Unfortunately, like most enchanting gifts, this transformation often comes at a cost – if a human male discovers a female selkie's seal skin, he can capture the creature. Without her seal coat, the selkie female cannot return to the water, so she is forced her to live on land as her abductor's wife.

Over the years, as these stories have been passed down from generation to generation, various versions of the tale have evolved.

In some versions of the legend, if a selkie wife is taken, she may buy back her seal skin and return to the sea to live with her fellow selkies, once she has produced human children for her husband.

In other versions, children which are born by a selkie are not truly human at all, but a mixture of the

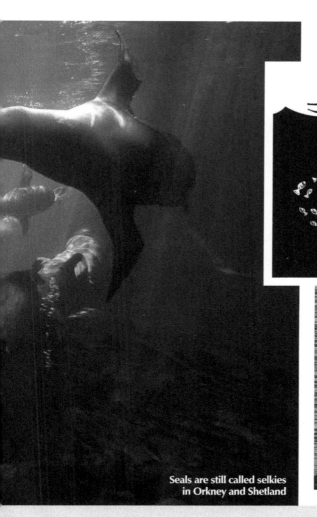

Seals are still called selkies
in Orkney and Shetland

**Left: Selkies must not lose
their seal skin**

**Below: They can disguise
themselves in human form**

"Selkie males are said to be flirtatious"

two beings, with human features and webbed hands and feet for swimming.

Like many mythological creatures, the male version gets off more lightly than the female of the species. While female selkies are often seized and kept against their will, selkie males are said to be flirtatious, often choosing to wed human women, although due to their unreliable personalities, those unions don't tend to last.

Causing a selkie physical harm, is said to have dire consequences. Legend has it that any person who kills a selkie and lets its blood drip into the sea, will trigger a fierce storm which will cause many a watery death.

In the northernmost of the Scottish islands, Orkney and Shetland, common seals are still referred to as selkies. ⊙

Words: DAWN GEDDES

BLOODTHIRSTY REDCAPS

Take care when exploring Scotland's ruined castles...

Terrifying redcap

MANY Scottish mythical beasts are mischievous, some are fairly benign, but others are downright malevolent.

Of all the supernatural stalkers or mythical creatures one could encounter while wandering a Scottish castle, the insatiable redcap demon is the most dreaded of all. Redcaps are gremlin-like ghouls or goblins who allegedly live in the Scottish Borders and get their name from the distinctive red hats that they wear.

These are dyed with human blood, and if a redcap fails to keep his cap freshly drenched, his life force withers away. Not being the largest or burliest of demons, they have a distinct hunger for solo travellers, and lie in wait amid the nooks and crannies of ruined castles until suitable prey wanders innocently in.

One particularly bloodthirsty redcap is said to inhabit the already ominous ruins of Hermitage Castle, a brooding titan of a fortress set deep within Liddesdale in the Scottish Borders, a place known as the bloodiest valley in Britain. What better hunting grounds than that?

Many a lone reiver – the colloquial name for someone from the Scottish Borders – and romantic wanderer is said to have fallen prey to Hermitage Castle's ghoulish guardian over the centuries. With an ever-increasing number of visitors exploring Scotland's castles the future for this Redcap seems bright red, indeed. O

"They have a hunger for solo travellers"

Hermitage Castle

Loch Ness

LOCH NESS MONSTER

Scotland's most famous monster draws tourists from the world over

MYTHS and legends surround almost all of Scotland's lochs. Whatever the source – whether it's the mist that clings to the glens and filled the imagination, ancient folklore passed down through generations, or real creatures lurking in the deeps – the tales make for fascinating reading.

Most popular of these myths, and most famous around the world, are the stories surrounding Scotland's largest loch, Loch Ness in the Highlands, and of Nessie, the monster who is said to inhabit it.

Rumours and stories of sightings have been reported for centuries, all the way back to Adomnán's account of St Columba who is said to have encountered the creature in AD565.

Eye-witnesses often describe her – yes, the general consensus is that Nessie is a she – as large in size with a long neck and one or more humps protruding from the water, leading to popular theories that the creature is a lone survivor of the Jurassic era. »

1934 photo of Nessie by London surgeon Robert Kenneth Wilson

The evidence for Nessie isn't just from eye-witness testimony, however. In 1954, sonar readings from a fishing boat detected something large keeping pace with the vessel in the depths below.

There have been many photographs claiming to show Nessie, the most famous of which was taken in 1934 by Robert Kenneth Wilson. It appears to show a long reptilian neck and head emerging from the water.

This photo was circulated around the world, and Nessie-hunters flocked to Loch Ness, eager to see the creature for themselves.

In 1993, however, further analysis of the photograph proved it to be a fake, created with a man-made Nessie head towed behind the boat.

Sturgeon

Many other photographs have been exposed as forgeries – or of large fish such as sturgeons or catfish – but there are still many who believe the Loch Ness Monster is real.

She was even the subject of a film, *Loch Ness*, in 1996 starring Ted Danson as a sceptical zoologist who eventually becomes a believer.

There have been many expeditions to search for Nessie, including a BBC-sponsored search in 2013 involving 600 sonar beams, which scanned the loch and could not find any large creatures.

In 2018, DNA analysis of the loch's water to identify any mysterious species, came up blank too. Interestingly, however, the study failed to find DNA evidence of any sturgeons or catfish either.

Left: Ted Danson in the film *Loch Ness*

Below: Looking for signs of life in 1934

Bottom: The 1954 sonar image said to be the best evidence of Nessie

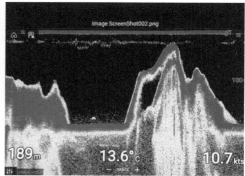

"She could be a surviving plesiosaur"

Theories about where Nessie came from and if she's real have been widely debated. It has been said she could be a surviving plesiosaur – an aquatic dinosaur – but the argument against this is that Loch Ness it too small to sustain a breeding population of plesiosaurs for such a long time.

Many agree it's impossible for a monster of such size to survive in Loch Ness, but there are those who still believe that Nessie is lurking somewhere in the loch.

Whatever the truth of the matter, many still spend hours scanning the loch for signs of life, with eight Nessie sightings reported in 2020. O

Words: KATRINA PATRICK

Legendary Scotland   57

MORAG OF MORAR

Sightings and folklore attest to a creature in Scotland's deepest loch

NESSIE isn't the only monster said to be lurking in Scotland's lochs. Loch Morar, in the Lochaber area of the Highlands, is home to Nessie's lesser-known cousin, Morag.

Morar is the deepest freshwater body in the British Isles, and is 310m (1017ft) at its deepest. The first recorded sighting of Morag was in 1887, and they have continued to the present day – though accounts differ. Some say the creature is a mermaid, some a plesiosaur-type creature like Nessie.

Alexander Carmichael, who collected local folklore at the turn of the 20th century, interviewed the inhabitants of the villages surrounding the loch, and wrote the following:

"There is a creature in Loch Morar and she is called Morag. She is never seen save when one of the hereditary people of the place dies. The last time she was seen was when Aeneas Macdonnell died in 1898. The Morag is peculiar to Loch Morar. She is seen in broad daylight and by many persons,

Morag is said to be a plesiosaur

including church persons. She appears in a black heap or ball slowing and deliberately rising in the water and moving along like a boat water-logged.

"The Morag is much disliked and is called by many uncomplimentary terms."

The sightings continued in the 20th century – in 1948 nine people in a boat claimed to have seen a creature measuring six metres (20ft).

Later, in 1969, two men claimed Morag had bumped into their boat, and only disappeared when they opened fire with a rifle and hit her with an oar. Things went quiet for a while and locals assumed Morag had succumbed to her wounds.

But a sighting in 2013 by holidaymakers, Doug and Charlotte Christie, confirmed the monster – or at least belief – was alive and well. ◯

"She appears in a black heap or ball rising in the water"

Swarms of bees can
be seen at odd times

CHRISTMAS BEES

Mystery around hives heading out to revel in seasonal festivities

I N the wee small hours of Christmas morning, bees in Scotland are said to leave their hives and swarm, before nonchalantly returning home as if nothing untoward has happened.

Over the centuries, many people have witnessed this curious sight, especially in north-east Scotland and Fife. Some bees even unite in a melodic hum on the stroke of midnight.

Though it's nice to think that the bees are overcome with Christmas spirit, it's much more likely that they're just out checking for danger.

A festive bee

In the olden days especially, many families were up and about much later than normal on Christmas Eve – out at Midnight Mass, or taking part in an abundance of Scottish yuletide traditions.

Bees are perceptive little souls, and they buzz around when something unexpected happens to disrupt their usual routine, which might explain their frenzied festive humming.

Or maybe they do just really love the holidays, and the bees are actually busy hanging up their teeny-tiny stockings for Santa. O

Words: LAURA BROWN

"Bees are overcome with Christmas spirit"

MYTHICAL BEASTS

Five more fabulous and sometimes fearsome beings

1 Highland Vampire

The baobhan sith is also known as the vampire of the Highlands. She appears as a beautiful young woman in a long green dress – but with deer hooves instead of feet. She is drawn to the scent of blood and preys on male hunters. She dances with them until they are exhausted, then drains their blood.

2 Nuckelavee

One of the most terrifying creatures in Scottish mythology is a demon from Orkney. He is part-horse and part-devil, with no skin to cover his yellow veins of black blood. His breath withers crops and infects livestock, and if you speak his name you better say a prayer in case he hears you. He can't cross running water, so if you see one – run for a stream.

3 House Elves

Brownies are small, nocturnal spirits who sneak into human houses and do chores while the occupants are asleep. They're also known as brùnaidh or gruagach in Scottish Gaelic. English versions sleep in the house, but Scottish brownies prefer to live near burns – small streams – out of sight behind waterfalls or under the heather.

4 The Wulver

This werewolf-like creature is said to stalk the moors of Shetland. Unlike werewolves, however, the wulver was never fully human, but born with a furred human body and a wolf's head. Much like wolves, he keeps to himself, and is only aggressive when threatened. He likes to fish, and will occasionally leave his catch on the windowsills of the poor.

5 Ghillie Dhu

This solitary fairy lives deep in the forests of the north-west Highlands. He is a kind-hearted mountain spirit with dark hair and clothes made from leaves. He is fond of children and appears to them more than adults, playing games and mischievous pranks with them. He can get very angry if adults trespass in his forest. His name comes from Ghillie, the Gaelic name for someone who looks after hunting and fishing parties on a country estate, and dubh, meaning black.○

Pictures: ©JOAN LLOPIS DOMÉNECH Words: KATRINA PATRICK

CELTIC

BEFORE the expansion of the Roman empire, most of Europe was dominated by Celtic peoples. The term Celtic generally refers to the culture of the European Iron Age, from around 1000BC onwards. Although some archaeologists argue that it could have originated as early as the Neolithic age which began around 10,000 years ago.

Today, six regions are considered Celtic nations, where the traditions, beliefs and languages of the ancient Celts have survived. These territories are Brittany in France, Cornwall in England, Wales, Ireland, the Isle of Man and Scotland. The Gaelic language – both Irish and Scottish – comes from the Celts.

Celtic art, which features intricate interwoven patterns, adorns many of Scotland's later standing stones, and influenced insular art of illuminated manuscripts like the *Book of Kells*.

Although much of Celtic mythology has been lost, evidence still exists across Scotland of their culture, beliefs and influence on the country. »

IN THE FOOTSTEPS OF KINGS

Kilmartin Glen is a historical hotbed of cairns, carvings and castles

KILMARTIN GLEN is a stunning historic location less than 50km (30 miles) south of Oban, with as many as 800 separate sites of interest.

The glen is one of the richest areas in Europe for prehistoric remains – including cairns, castles, forts, megaliths, stone circles and carvings – but among them, Dunadd Fort is one of the most interesting.

Signs of human activity remain at the fort's site, some dating back more than 2000 years, yet there is little left to suggest to the untrained eye that a full citadel once stood atop the modest hill.

By the time the Romans left Britain, around 410CE, the area now known as Argyll was a kingdom in its own right named Dál Riata – inhabited by Gaels, from whom we get the Gaelic language.

Records from the seventh century tell us that Dunadd was the capital of Dál Riata and the seat of Gaelic kings for around 300 years.

The most prominent bits of evidence are a basin, smooth and round, carved into a rock in the ground. Nearby are two separate carved footprints, and it is thought that these were used during inauguration ceremonies for new kings, symbolising the new ruler's dominion over the land.

Words: SAM LEWIS

The well at Dunadd

"Symbolising the new ruler's dominion"

The path to the top of Dunadd Fort

Etched into the rock here are an image of a boar and an inscription in the early Medieval alphabet of Ogham. High-quality pottery, weapons and other metalwork have also been found – in some of the greatest quantities and varieties anywhere in Europe.

Viking raids from the Atlantic Sea and constant battles with the Picts from the north east saw an end to the kingdom of Dál Riata around 900CE, and an abandonment of Dunadd.

Today, while little remains in the way of walls, visitors have the chance to stand where the Gaelic kings stood, and to look out across Kilmartin Glen – drinking in thousands of years of human history. O

LIBRARY OF IONA

Lost treasure trove of knowledge could be hidden in Inner Hebrides

IN the 1950s, a team of archaeology students from the University of St Andrews started digging on the Treshnish Isles, near Mull.

They were searching for buried treasure – the lost Library of Iona. Alas, they didn't find it, but many people still believe a whole world of knowledge is hiding somewhere in the Inner Hebrides.

Some can't agree on whose library they're searching for, though – perhaps the ancient books of the Druids or St Columba's monastic manuscripts?

Before St Columba landed on Iona in 563CE, turning it into the cradle of Christianity in Scotland, the island sometimes went by the name Innis nam Druidneach, or Isle of Druids.

The druids, a Celtic name for those who practice magic or religion, are said to have founded a great library there, containing an incredibly vast collection of books nabbed by King Fergus II after the sack of Rome in 410CE.

But the history books are a little hazy – and sadly there is no concrete proof of a hidden Druid library on Iona or nearby.

However, there's the possibility that the subsequent monastery library's books were buried to protect them from Vikings.

The Book Of Kells, thought to have been produced by the monks of Iona, survived and was taken to Ireland, but it's not known whether the rest of the books were destroyed, spirited away or hidden on Iona or the Treshnish Isles.

The missing library might never be found – indeed, it might not even exist – but archaeologists live in hope that it might one day resurface. ○

The Book Of Kells

"Buried to protect them from Vikings"

THE CAILLEACH

The Queen of Winter bathes in a whirlpool and dictates the season

THE elemental power of Scotland's old Celtic gods is embodied by the Cailleach – pronounced kah-lee-ack.

She has many names – the Veiled One and Beira, the Queen of Winter among them – and according to Gaelic lore it was she who raised the mountains of the Highlands, guards the creatures of the glens, and heralds the coming of the deathly frosts of winter.

Known in legends and folktales across Scotland, Ireland and the Isle of Man, the Cailleach is at once mother, guardian, tyrant, and creator, whose whims are as unpredictable as the land itself.

The Cailleach carries a hammer

She is a goddess, yet unlike monotheistic gods who inhabit a distinct plane from mortals, she is as much a part of our world as the winds and waters that define life in Scotland. She carries a hammer for shaping the hills and valleys, and is said to be the mother of all the goddesses and gods in Celtic mythology.

Worshipped and feared wherever the Gaels made their homes, she lives in the high places among stone and sky.

At Samhain, October 31, she descends to the Corryvreckan whirlpool off the Isle of Jura to wash her great plaid in the maelstrom. The Corryvreckan is the third largest **》**

The Corryvreckan

Ice crystals

whirlpool in the world. Flood tides and inflow from the Firth of Lorne to the west can drive the waters of Corryvreckan to waves of more than 9.1m (30 feet), and the roar of the resulting maelstrom can be heard 16km (10 miles) away – it is said that this maelstrom is at its worst when the Cailleach washes her plaid.

Once she is finished the laundry, she hangs her great plaid up to dry. Ice crystals drift from it to cover the land in cold, bringing on the winter season.

Là Fhèill Brìghde, or Bride's Day is the first day of spring in the Gaelic calendar on February 1. This is the day that the Cailleach gathers her firewood for the rest of the winter. Legend has it that if she intends to make the winter last much longer, she will make the weather

Beinn na Caillich

The stones are still moved each year

"At Beltane the Gaels must rebel against her icy rule"

bright and sunny on February 1, so she can gather plenty of firewood to keep herself warm during the coming months.

As a result, if Là Fhèill Brìghde is a day of foul weather it means the Cailleach is asleep, and will soon run out of firewood, meaning winter is almost over.

At Beltane on May 1, the Gaels must rebel against her icy rule with bonfires to make way for Angus and Bride, the King and Queen of Summer.

Forced to retreat she awaits the inevitable return of Samhain from her stronghold, the location of which varies depending on who you're speaking to. Popular locations include Ben Cruachan, Glen Nevis, and Beinn na Caillich on Skye. O

Cailleach's Shelter

In Gleann Cailliche at Glen Lyon in Perthshire there is a stream named Allt Cailliche which runs into Loch Lyon. It is home to the oldest continuous Celtic ritual in the UK. In the glen there's a tiny shieling, known as known as Tigh nan Cailleach – Scottish Gaelic for "house of the old women".

The shieling shelters a group of small tapered stones representing the Cailleach, her husband the Bodach, and her family. Local legend claims that the Cailleach and the Bodach were once given shelter by locals, and while they stayed there raising their children the glen was prosperous.

When they left, they gave the locals the stones, with the promise that as long as the stones were taken outside to keep watch over the glen during the summer, and kept safe indoors over winter, the glen would continue to be fertile.

For thousands of years they have been brought in and out from their holdfast at Samhain and Beltane respectively. The last named custodian of the Cailleach was shepherd Bob Bissett as recorded in the 1970s, and though he has since passed away the ceremony is upheld by hands unknown to this very day.

Words: DAVID WEINCZOK

LAND OF GIANTS

Legends say colossal rivals' fearsome battles changed Scotland

S TORIES of giants can be found in both Scotland and Ireland – in surviving Celtic mythology and also in the names of places.

The island of Staffa, in the Inner Hebrides in Scotland, has the same strange and remarkable geometric rock formations as the Giant's Causeway in Northern Ireland, and it is thought that the two were once connected by an ancient lava flow.

If Celtic legends are to be believed, however, the rocks are all that remains of a bridge built by giants. The Irish warrior, Fionn mac Cumhaill, challenged the Scottish giant Benandonner to a duel, and built the bridge so the giant could reach him.

When Benandonner came charging across the bridge, Fionn realised he could never win against him and hid in a cradle, disguised as a baby.

Benandonner found the cradle, remarked on the baby's size – and promptly ran back across the bridge in fear of how big the baby's father must be.

Left: The Giant's Causeway, Northern Ireland

The Old Man of Storr

The island of Staffa

"Rocks are the remains of a giant's bridge"

As he ran, he smashed the bridge into the sea so Fionn couldn't follow. All that remains are the two strange rock formations on either side of the Irish Sea.

Giants usually come in pairs in the stories, and Scotland is full of tales of rivals who live on opposing hills, and spend their days hurling boulders across the glen, river or sea that divides them.

Across the country you'll find erratics – rocks borne to their final resting place by glaciers thousands of years ago. To the Celtic people these huge boulders were evidence of fearsome battles between giants.

Another legend says that a colossal giant once lived in Trotternish Ridge on the Isle of Skye. His family buried him on the ridge when he died, but left his thumb sticking out of the ground as a marker – creating the Old Man of Storr. ○

Words: KATRINA PATRICK

FACES OF STONE

Step back to the time of Druids at Dunino Den Pagan ritual site

DUNINO PARISH CHURCH near St Andrews is just unassuming enough to guard its secrets from all but the most inquisitive explorers.

Nothing, at first, gives away that it is one of the oldest and most important ritual sites in Scotland.

A small stone altar in the kirkyard always overflowing with coins is the first sign that there is more to this den than meets the eye.

Pass through the veil of trees beyond the stone and the den is revealed. A stone promontory with a sacred and impenetrably murky well lies before you, where a mysterious carved face watches from the red-leaved tree, bringing the weirwood trees in *Game of Thrones* to mind.

The pool at Dunino serves as a liminal place believed by the ancient Celts to be a gateway to the Otherworld.

Descend down a stone-cut stair past several carved crosses – some from the eighth century, and some far more modern – and you may get the uneasy feeling that you are being watched. You are.

Amid offerings to the faerie folk tied to tree branches and the gentle current of the Dunino Burn is a face carved into the stone wall of the den. It is bearded, with deep-set eyes and an expression somewhere between fury and wisdom. O

Offerings left at the site

A rock carving

Words: DAVID WEINCZOK

"Mysterious carved faces watch over the den"

The face at Dunino

CELTS TO CHRISTIANS

Many modern traditions reflect earlier practices

Duddingston Loch

E VEN the grandest cathedral would seem like little more than a gilded cage in the eyes of Scotland's Celtic, pre-Christian peoples.

With the exception of megalithic monuments such as standing stones and cairns, their spiritual centres were not man-made structures but natural settings such as groves, pools, islands, caves, clearings and bogs.

These are all places of transition, liminal realms where they believed the veil between our world and the Celtic Otherworld was thinnest.

Bogs and pools seem to have been especially significant as places of sacrifice. Several bodies as well as large hoards of deliberately broken or offered

metal weaponry and luxury items have been recovered from locations like Cladh Hallan on South Uist and Duddingston Loch in Edinburgh.

The slow entrenchment of Christianity in Scotland from the fifth century did little to alter people's belief that the world was inhabited and influenced by what we could call magical and supernatural beings.

Medieval Scots saw no contradiction between being devout Christians and leaving offerings for the faerie folk who lived at the local burn or small stream – an undeniably pagan practice.

Celtic rituals and festivals follow the natural cycle of the seasons upon which the lives of all people and animals balance. »

"Women would flock to Arthur's Seat at first light on May Day"

Some Gaelic festivals echoed by Christian celebrations are Yule and Ostara, the traditions of which have been adopted into the Christian celebrations of Christmas and Easter.

Some have translated less fluidly, such as Imbolc, which celebrated the pregnancy of ewes, but we do often undertake a "spring clean", an Imbolc custom recorded since at least the 10th century.

Since the Gaelic world beyond its clergy did not utilise the written word, the lore of a clan was entrusted to bards and seannachies – a Highland bard.

Spring cleaning is related to lambing

They committed history, legends, and genealogy to memory going back generations to the mythical age of heroes and giants. Like those who worked metal, seannachies were regarded as being closest among mortals to the divine and were referred to as the aos-dana, "the folk of gifts".

Sitting around a castle's hearth or among the hillside heather on a moonlit night, even well into the 18th-century bards would recount tales of faerie folk or water beasts like kelpies with the same earnestness that they would use to relay the results of the last cattle raid or clan feud.

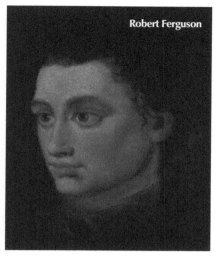

Robert Ferguson

It's customary
to bring coal
to first foot

After all, both the natural and the supernatural – though they would not have acknowledged that distinction – were part of the rhythm of daily life.

Attaining good or bad fortune was a serious preoccupation for medieval and early modern Scots, and often for modern ones, too.

First-footing is perhaps the best-known example, where the first foot across your threshold on the new year can bring good or bad fortune for the year ahead.

If it belongs to a tall, dark-haired gentleman, it's a blessing, but if he's blonde or red-haired, however, it's a curse. This is perhaps a leftover from the Viking raids of the eighth to the 13th century.

The first footer should also bear gifts – preferably coal

to heat the home, a silver coin for prosperity, a tipple of whisky for a little temporal pleasure and a black bun and salt with which to partake in guest-right. This was an ancient custom whereby host and guest eat bread and salt together to represent a sacred promise not to harm one another.

Another ancient rite of fortune is still observed in Edinburgh. Dew was the most sacred form of water for the Celts, prized for its restorative powers, and as recently as the last century young women would flock to Arthur's Seat at first light on May Day to wash their faces in the morning dew. This bestowed vitality, happiness, and above all beauty for the year to come.

Though the number of participants is now a trickle, **»**

Beltane Fire Festival

Samhain Festival

Words: DAVID WEINCZOK

"Celebrates light and life after the winter"

the custom has been immortalised by Robert Ferguson in his poem, *Auld Reekie*, in 1773.

> On May-day, in a fairy ring,
> We've seen them round St Anthon's spring,
> Frae grass the cauler dew draps wring
> To weet their een,
> And water clear as crystal spring
> To synd them clean

The most famous two festivals in Celtic mythology that are still celebrated by some today are Beltane and Samhain. Beltane, on the last eve of April, celebrates the return of light and life after the darkness and death of winter.

Samhain, Summer's End, is Beltane's opposite on the great and eternal Wheel of the Year, marking the last harvest and the beginning of hardship.

Both Samhain and Beltane are still marked across Scotland in ceremonies ranging from small, personal devotions to massive fire festivals in Edinburgh attended by thousands. O

TOP SUPERSTITIONS

From warding off witches to bringing luck and health

1 Wild Fire

No firewood, coal or peat were to be shared between houses on the first day of every quarter of the Gaelic year – New Year's Day, St Bride's Day, Beltane and Lammas. It was believed that by dividing the fire, you divided the health of the livestock, weakening the herd.

2 Right-Hand Turn

It was believed all things should be done in a left to right motion to follow the sun. Screws were turned this way, coffins were turned into the grave to the right, and it was unlucky to get out of bed on the left – which is where "getting out of bed on the wrong side" comes from.

3 White Heather

Purple heather is very common in Scotland, but less so is the lucky white heather. In a Celtic legend dating from the third century, Malvina, daughter of warrior-poet Ossian, cried for her lover lost in battle. Her tears supposedly turned the heather white, and she prayed that it would bring good fortune to all that found it.

4 Blessing The House

It was customary to put a cat's claw, a man's nail and a cow's hoof below the foundation of every newly built house, and a piece of silver would be placed under the door post. New arrivals would burn straw upon entering, called a sop-seilbhe – possession or spittle wisp.

5 Wards Against Evil

There are many devices believed to ward off witches, but the rowan tree is a particular favourite and planting one in your garden is believed to provide protection against witches. Sprigs of  rowan were also carried for protection and tied round the necks of livestock. This old superstition was taken with Scottish emigrants to New Zealand, where rowans are still commonly found growing outside suburban houses in Dunedin. O

Words: KATRINA PATRICK

GHOSTS

△

IN old Scottish folklore you'll hear tales of the "thin places" where it is believed the veil between this world and the "other" world, or afterlife, is thin.

"Heaven and earth," as a Celtic saying goes, "are only three feet apart, but in thin places that distance is even shorter."

Many believed that the thin places are where those long dead can pass back through that veil and into the world of the living.

Ghost sightings have frequently been reported at many of Scotland's thin places, and at scenes of traumatic deaths.

At the locations of bloody battles and gruesome murders, the victims' spirits are said to linger on – either to warn visitors of the danger, or to exact revenge.

Read on to discover some of Scotland's most spine-chilling stories, most haunted houses and ghostly sightings from across the centuries... »

A CURSED CASTLE

Haunting follows Lord Fyvie's deadly quest for an heir

ACCORDING to legend, 13th-century bard and seer Thomas the Rhymer appeared at Fyvie Castle's door requesting shelter.

When this was denied him, he placed a curse on the castle that it would never pass in direct line between more than two generations.

Fast forward a few centuries to 1599 when Lord Fyvie, Alexander Seton, was frustrated that his marriage to Lillias Drummond was producing no sons, only daughters. Women could not inherit property at that time, so it seemed Thomas's curse was still active.

Unfortunately, Lord Fyvie blamed his wife, rather than the curse for the lack of male heirs, and promptly began an affair with Lillias's cousin.

Lillias died soon after, but stories differ on how this came about. Some say that Lillias learned of the affair and died of a broken heart, but many say her husband starved her to death in the castle's tower for failing to produce a male heir for him.

Lord Fyvie then married Lillias's cousin, Grizel, but on their wedding night, ghostly wails were heard outside the bedchamber window. In the morning servants found the name D. LILLIAS DRUMMOND etched into the stone windowsill, which can still be seen to this day.

Fyvie Castle

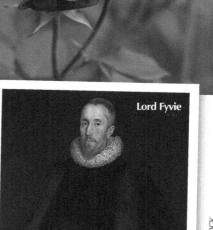

The ghost leaves a scent of roses

Lord Fyvie

Words: KATRINA PATRICK

"He starved her to death in the tower"

Lord Fyvie's second marriage didn't last long either after two daughters and a son who died in infancy. Grizel died in 1606, again under suspicious circumstances, and Lord Fyvie married again, and finally raised a son who would inherit his estate.

But what happened to Grizel?

A story is also told that in 1920 during renovation work, a skeletal woman was discovered behind a bedroom wall. On the day her remains were laid to rest in Fyvie cemetery, the castle residents started to be plagued by strange noises and unexplained occurrences.

Fearing he had offended the deceased woman, this castle's Laird had the skeleton exhumed and replaced behind the bedroom wall, at which point the haunting ceased.

Was this the body of Lillias, starved to death in the tower? Or that of her cousin, Grizel?

We may never know, but to this day a grey lady is said to walk the halls of Fyvie Castle, leaving behind the scent of roses. O

HORRIBLE HISTORY

Leith Hall's grim past has provided an array of ghostly goings-on

Entrance to Leith Hall

LEITH HALL in Aberdeenshire definitely makes the rankings for one of Scotland's creepiest castles. Behind its foreboding entrance lie large rooms that visitors say feel inexplicably claustrophobic, with sudden drops in temperature, strange smells and presences.

Several ghosts of the Leith family have been sighted over the years, but the one most frequently reported is that of John Leith III.

After a drunken brawl in Archie Campbell's Tavern in Aberdeen in 1763, John was shot in the head. He was brought home, but died three days later on Christmas Day. It is said his spirit lingers, moaning in pain with a bloodied bandage around his eyes.

Guests have reported seeing him in their bed chambers, and several reported nightmares about a face bending over them while they slept.

But he's not the only ghost that walks the eerie grounds of Leith Hall.

An episode of TV show *Most Haunted* was filmed here in 2003, and researchers discovered that a strange-looking tree in the garden was used by the lairds for executions – the scars left by the hanging rope are still visible on its branches.

During the First World War, Leith Hall became a temporary hospital for more than 500 wounded soldiers shipped back from France and Belgium.

The smell of camphor still lingers in some of the rooms – despite a century of cleaning – and the ghosts of men in military uniforms are still seen by visitors. ○

Leith Hall

Words: KATRINA PATRICK

CITY OF THE DEAD

Greyfriars Kirkyard in Edinburgh is claimed to be one of the most haunted places in the UK

NO one can say for sure just how many dead lie in the soil of Greyfriars Kirkyard in Edinburgh's Old Town, but between 1562 when Mary, Queen of Scots, established the kirkyard and 1900 the figure has been estimated at 100,000.

The vast majority of those died of illness and the miseries of poverty, and could not afford the dignity of a casket. They were piled in mass graves, with many human remains now lying less than an arm's length below the topsoil.

Little wonder, then, that Greyfriars is consistently

Skull and crossbones

ranked among the most haunted locations in Britain.

There are also a morbidly fascinating array of murals and monuments in the kirkyard, with the motif of a skull and crossbones waiting to spook you around every bend.

These are not the graves of pirates, nor are they intended to frighten you. Instead, the often visceral depictions of the dead, alongside innocent looking cherubs, are reminders that death awaits us all. It's not an especially uplifting place.

Some of the most striking carvings can be found on the the gravestone of James Borthwick, »

A mortsafe to protect remains

Inside a mausoleum

"MacKenzie stalks the kirkyard searching for souls to torment"

against the eastern wall of the kirk. Borthwick was a surgeon who died in 1840, and his gravestone is decorated with carved surgical instruments such as syringes and bone chisels alongside an alarmingly lifelike skeleton – reminders of Edinburgh Medical College's role as a beacon for the study of medicine and anatomy.

This expertise was made possible by a steady supply of cadavers disinterred by grave robbers from the city's kirkyards in the 17th to 18th centuries. This is why there

are cages over some graves, known as mortsafes, to stop folk digging up bodies to sell to the college.

There are many tales of one culprit who seems to be responsible for the majority of the ghostly accounts at Greyfriars Kirkyard – Bluidy Mackenzie.

Sir George Mackenzie – c.1636-1691 – had a penchant for summary executions before any trial could take place, which earned him his grisly epithet.

Under his supervision upwards of 1000 Covenanters,

Covenanters were persecuted

Greyfriar's Bobby

Bluidy Mackenzie

Greyfriars Bobby

No account of Greyfriars Kirkyard would be complete without a stop to greet the statue of Greyfriars Bobby, a 19th-century Skye terrier known as Edinburgh's best friend. His master was John Gray, a night watchman who sought a canine companion. John died of tuberculosis in 1858 and was buried in the kirkyard. It is said Bobby stood vigil at his master's grave for 14 years. He was cared for by locals who would bring food to the kirkyard gates every day at the firing of the One O'Clock Gun. Some details have surely been embellished over the years, but, regardless, little Bobby has found an enduring place in the city's heart.

who rebelled against the monarchy's influence over the church, were held in a roofless prison in appalling conditions, and the chained-off area of the kirkyard where this occurred – a stone's throw from Mackenzie's mausoleum – has sent many a self-proclaimed psychic and medium running from the ground in terror.

Mackenzie is said to stalk the kirkyard searching for the souls of Covenanters to torment. By Robert Louis Stevenson's time, the legend of Bluidy Mackenzie was so firmly entrenched in Edinburgh's psyche, he wrote in 1897, "When a man's soul is certainly in hell, his body will scarce lie quiet in a tomb however costly; sometime or other the door must open, and the reprobate come forth in the abhorred garments of the grave".

Accounts of Mackenzie's wrath range from people being forcefully pushed, having sudden onsets of extreme terror, and even discovering inexplicable scratches on their bodies after leaving the kirkyard. O

Words: DAVID WEINCZOK

PHANTOM PIPERS

Ghostly notes of trapped pipers echo through Scotland's castles

R UMOURS of mysterious tunnels running beneath Scottish castles are as common as midges in June. Not all are nefarious though. One, for instance, is said to simply provide swift and secret passage between Blackness Castle and the House of the Binns.

But then, there is the tunnel beneath Yester Castle in East Lothian, blocked up by terrified locals convinced that it led to a "Hell Mouth".

There is one story that appears again and again in Scotland – that of the trapped phantom bagpiper.

The most famous version is at Edinburgh Castle. Tunnels were apparently discovered leading from the castle towards Holyrood Palace, and a young

Dunskey Castle

piper was sent into them to discover their extent. He walked into the tunnel, playing his pipes, with the rest of the group following safely above ground. Halfway along the Royal Mile the sound of his pipes below the cobbles went silent, and for fear of what took him the tunnel entrance was sealed.

A variation on the ghostly piper tale has the doomed soul bring a canine companion with them, only for the man to vanish and the dog to reappear with all its hair plucked or singed away. The meaning of this would not have been lost on the deeply superstitious Scots of the 18th century – the pair had encountered the devil himself.

Another phantom piper can be heard beneath Dunskey Castle near Stranraer. Its 14th-century laird Walter de Curry, described as a "sea rover", captured a rival piper and humiliated the man by forcing him to

Edinburgh Castle

Above: Yester Castle ruins

Right: There are many tales of phantom pipers

serve as his jester. The piper didn't suffer this indignity quietly and was sentenced to starve in the dungeons for his outspokenness, with only his pipes for company. Desperate for freedom he followed a tunnel that seemed to lead to a seaside cave, but never emerged.

Intriguingly, workers in 1911 found a large, cavernous space in the sea cliffs where an eerie tune plays. Whether it's a whistle of the wind or the forlorn tune of the proud piper is for you to decide. O

"His pipes below the cobbles went silent"

Words: DAVID WEINCZOK

It's said Fenella used a witch's brew

A ROYAL MURDER

Dramatic tale of a revenge killing created legend of Fenella

THE Den of Fenella is said to be haunted by a ghost in purgatory for killing the king. Legends such as this are an essential part of Scottish culture and St Cyrus, a small community in Aberdeenshire, has more tales to tell than most.

The tale which explains the name of The Den of Fenella has all the ingredients of a great story – a young, beautiful noblewoman kills the King of Scotland for reasons shrouded in mystery, and is hounded to her death by vengeful horsemen.

The den is a deep, overgrown gully, stretching downwards from the edge of the Aberdeen road,

Kenneth II

north of St Cyrus, to the shore. This dangerous but beautiful place is said to be haunted by the ghost of the tragic beauty from whom the den takes its name.

Fenella's story has been well documented in Scottish history, but it has become part legend over the years have gone by.

She was the beautiful young wife of a north-east thane, or noble. Kenneth II was on the throne of Scotland at the time Fenella attended the royal court with her husband in 995CE.

One day, Kenneth was brutally murdered and evidence was said to point to Fenella as the culprit. It

The dangerous gorge

"*Horsemen hunted her down when the murder was discovered*"

is said that Kenneth had killed her only son, and grief drove her to vengeance.

Stories vary about how she did the deed – some say she was a witch, who brewed a poison from herbs gathered in the Garvock Forest.

Others claim she created a "mechanical device", which fired an arrow into the king's heart when he entered his private chamber, while another story suggested she had made sure of his death by using both methods.

The years have hidden her reasons, as the haar hides the trail she took to escape the horsemen who hunted her down when the King's murder was discovered.

They pursued her across the Howe of the Mearns, over the hill which now bears her name – Strath Fenella – down to St Cyrus where, to avoid capture, she threw herself to her death in the deep, dark gully.

From that day on the gorge became known as the Den of Fenella. Only the brave venture down its steep and treacherous slopes – who knows what lies hiding in wait at the bottom. O

Words: JEAN ROSS ANDERSON

FAIRYTALE CASTLE OF PHANTOMS

Beautiful Crathes Castle hosts at least
two spooky spirits from a haunted history

"Workers found skeletal remains of a young woman and infant."

CONSIDERING the battles, murders, conspiracies, and tragedies that unfolded within the walls of Scotland's castles, it is no wonder that so many are believed to be haunted.

One of the most beloved and well-documented of these ghosts is the Green Lady of Crathes Castle in Aberdeenshire.

At first glance Crathes does not seem a particularly spooky place. Its resplendent gardens and pink hue would be better suited to a Disney fable than a tale of terror.

Yet Crathes' fairytale facade hides a sinister past. A ghostly lady has been seen floating through the castle, often holding a baby, and with a distinctly green tinge.

The castle dates from the 16th century, and the Burnett family, who are still in residence, were granted the land by Robert the Bruce in 1323. The land was boggy, yet the Burnetts were determined to build a castle there. Many generations of Burnetts attempted to drain the loch and alter their surroundings, and some speculate that nature itself rose up in retaliation.

During renovations in the 19th century, workers were shocked to find the skeletal remains of a young woman and infant. They were buried beneath the hearthstone of the fireplace in what would become »

The Green Lady haunts the castle

known as the Green Lady's Room. While no one knows the identity of the child – or the spectral woman in green – the story seems to have a pedigree dating to at least the 18th century.

In around 1746, the year of the Battle of Culloden, Alexander Burnett, 4th Baronet of Crathes, attempted to drain the loch surrounding his ancient home of Leys several miles from Crathes Castle.

His son was killed in the attempt and family records state the Green Lady began to appear to him shortly after this loss. The Baronet developed an obsessive fear of ghosts – was she trying to confide in another who had felt the pain of losing a child?

"She is an echo of a tragedy, not of terror"

The castle's walled garden

The tower

It is notable that the Green Lady has never acted maliciously or brought harm to any who see her. She is an echo of a tragedy, not of terror.

Still, that does not prevent the castle's staff from being spooked. Sudden drops in temperature, a feeling of being watched, and strange noises of someone walking around after opening hours are frequently reported by its caretakers.

Queen Victoria stayed at Crathes on several occasions, and was among those who witnessed the Green Lady pacing back and forth in front of the fireplace.

Much more recently, during a family visit to Crathes in 2016, Bill Andrew snapped a photograph of his daughter, granddaughter, and great-grandson posing in front of the tower. Later, when he was looking at the photograph, he discovered that his family were not alone.

An unusual tangible figure can be seen standing behind them in the castle's entrance, wearing a simple, wide dress typical of the 17th and 18th centuries with what appears to be a hood or veil, almost as though she were in mourning.

The Green Lady's sorrow, it seems, shall be a part of Crathes Castle's story for many years to come. O

Murderer Or Victim?

There is another female ghost said to frequent Crathes Castle, but the jury is out on whether she was the murderer or the victim in this tragic tale.

In the 16th century, Baronet Alexander Burnett – there were many Alexanders in this family – married the ambitious Agnes Lechtoun. The story goes that he died suddenly and suspiciously leaving Agnes to run the estate in guardianship for their young son, who was called – you've guessed it – Alexander.

When the son came of age Agnes made plans for his marriage that would heighten their power. The young Alexander, however, had fallen for another woman, Bertha.

Bertha didn't fit with Agnes's plans and she poisoned her in the tower room of Crathes Castle, but died suddenly herself on the anniversary of the murder – just as suspicion was beginning to turn on her.

Over the years visitors have reported a female ghost in the tower, now named the White Lady. Whether she is Agnes or Bertha we will never know, but she reappears on the anniversary of the murder.

Words: DAVID WEINCZOK

Lochan nan Corp

LOCH OF THE DEAD

Mysterious lights seen over the water after deadly funeral accident

HIDDEN in the middle of the Loch Lomond and The Trossachs National Park lies Lochan nan Corp, or "the little loch of the dead".

It's situated near the top of Ben Ledi on the Old Coffin Road from Glen Finglas to St Bride's Chapel, where the notorious 17th-century outlaw Rob Roy MacGregor is buried, close to Loch Lubnaig.

In days of old, locals would carry the coffin of their beloved on their shoulders from their homes in Glen Finglas over Ben Ledi to the chapel for burial.

Some think the lochan is named because of its proximity to Bealach nan Corp, the Pass of the Dead, which is the highest point on the route.

But some say its sinister name refers to an accident more than 100 years ago in the depths of winter. A funeral party of 200 mourners from Glen Finglas were crossing Ben Ledi on their way to St Bride's Chapel, so the tale goes.

They became lost on the bealach, began crossing the frozen lochan, and all 200 plunged to their deaths when the ice cracked.

Walkers on Ben Ledi have occasionally reported sightings of lights near the loch, which some believe to be the lanterns of the lost funeral party, still trying to find their way home. O

"They began crossing the frozen loch"

MOST HAUNTED

Discover the top Scottish places besieged by ghosts

1 Skaill House
Orkney

This 17th-century Orcadian mansion was built in the grounds of the Neolithic village of Skara Brae. In the 1990s, Norse skeletons were found under the floorboards and over the years visitors have reported sightings of ghostly figures and odd occurrences like the sudden waft of tobacco smoke.

2 Eilean Donan
Kyle of Lochalsh

An 18th-century soldier still wanders the halls of this eerie and majestic castle. It's said he was one of the Spanish soldiers stationed here during the Jacobite Rising of 1719, and was killed in a siege. The ghost of Lady Mary has also been witnessed by many visitors in one of the castle's bedrooms.

3 Glamis Castle
Glamis

The childhood home of the Queen Mother has more than its fair share of resident ghosts. Guests have been awoken by sounds of screaming or the sight of an armoured knight leaning over their beds. A grey lady has been seen walking through walls in the castle's chapel and the ghost of young serving girl runs through the grounds.

4 Culloden Moor
Culloden

On April 16, 1746, the last pitched battle in Britain took place on Culloden Moor. It was a bloody defeat for the Jacobite army loyal to Prince Charles Edward Stuart, and it is said that the Jacobite dead return on the anniversary. Battle cries and clashing of swords have been heard, and it is believed no birds sing over the battlefield.

5 Dunrobin Castle
Golspie

A young woman is said to haunt the Seamstress's Room of Dunrobin Castle, where visitors and staff have reported hearing strange crying. The story goes that in the 15th century the Earl of

Sutherland imprisoned the daughter of a rival clan laird in this room, with plans to force her to marry him so he could wield power over the clan lands. The woman knotted her bed sheets into a rope and tried to escape out of the window, but sadly fell to her death. O

Words: KATRINA PATRICK

ANCIENTS
△

CARVINGS, cairns and stone circles can be found across Scotland, created by the country's earliest inhabitants.

People have lived in Scotland since pre-historic times, with the earliest evidence of human settlers in the country found in Biggar, South Lanarkshire.

Flint tools were uncovered there, carbon dated to 12,000BCE. This discovery was a breakthrough – it is the only evidence of human settlers to predate the last glacial period in Scotland. This was known as the Loch Lomond Readvance when ice and intensely cold conditions scoured the country.

Most remains left by Scotland's ancient settlers are dated after the Loch Lomond Readvance, when the glaciers retreated around 9500BCE.

In many cases only stone has stood the test of time, and the stone circles these ancient people erected continue to inspire and bewitch visitors.

Discover some of these ancient and mysterious sites on the following pages... »

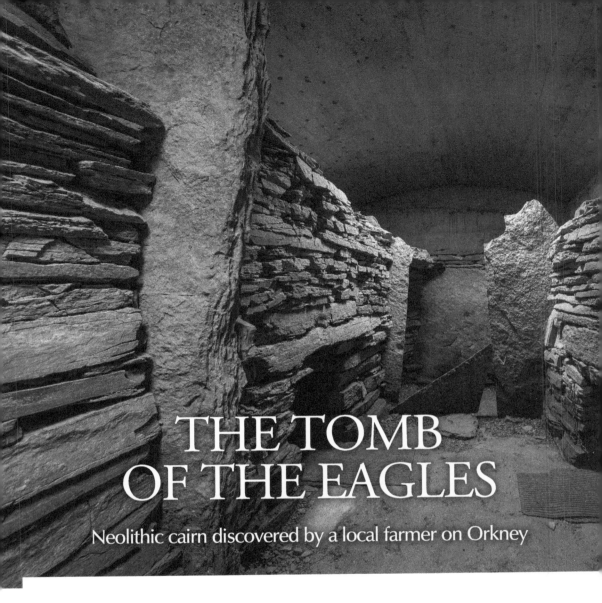

THE TOMB
OF THE EAGLES

Neolithic cairn discovered by a local farmer on Orkney

THE Tomb of the Eagles, also known as the Isbister Chambered Cairn, sits above the cliffs on the south coast of the Orkney island of South Ronaldsay.

A Neolithic cairn, The Tomb of the Eagles acted as a burial ground from around 3000BCE. Despite its ancient history, the cairn was only discovered by chance in 1958 by local farmer Ronnie Simison.

A small excavation of the tomb was started by Ronnie, who discovered a number of bones, 30 human skulls and artefacts including a mace head, a button and a knife made of chert – a hard, fine-grained rock, similar to flint.

In Ronnie's initial excavation, he also discovered the remains of at least 14 white-tailed eagles, the largest bird of prey in the UK, which led the cairn to be christened The Tomb of the Eagles.

A full excavation began 18 years later in 1976,

A skull discovered at the site

The narrow entrance

Pictures: NICK DRAINEY Words: SCOTT PATERSON

"The remains of 14 white-tailed eagles"

which led to the discovery of more than 16,000 human bones. The bones found were studied by Judson T Chesterman of the University of Sheffield's Archaeology department, who estimated them to belong to around 342 people.

The Tomb of the Eagles sits mere miles from a Bronze Age site, the Liddle Burnt Mound, which Ronnie Simison also discovered, and is just one of many locations which hark back to Orkney's rich and exciting Neolithic history. O

MAGICAL MOOR

Arran's Machrie stone circles thought to power Electric Brae

A SEEMINGLY normal road in Ayrshire with an unexplained optical illusion has been puzzling both residents and tourists for centuries.

The Electric Brae, or Croy Brae as it's known locally, is a bizarre stretch of road which makes your car look as if it is being rolled uphill, when it's actually going down.

The phenomenon was named Electric Brae by the Victorians, who were fascinated by the invention of electricity. Stumped by the anomaly, locals at the time concluded a power source on the nearby Isle of Arran must be pulling vehicles upwards by magnetic force.

Arran is known as "Scotland in miniature" for its dramatic and varied geography. It's a place of golden beaches, shaded glens and rugged mountains and its highest point, Goat Fell at 874 metres (2867 feet), makes for a challenging climb.

On the west coast of Arran is the village of Machrie, home to the Machrie Moor stone circles – 11 separate sites, surrounded by the remains of generations of stone huts and more primitive constructions.

People have lived in the area for at least 8000 years, but work began on the circles in about 3500BCE. They

"It was these ancient structures that were believed to be causing the phenomenon"

were originally dug as pits, before tall wooden posts were used to erect timber circles. The stone circles appeared in approximately 2000BCE, and it was these ancient structures that modern-day locals believed was causing the phenomenon on the mainland.

Circles One and Two are the most impressive, with one of the stones topping 5.5m (18ft), though many of their tall red sandstone pillars have now fallen. Circle Five is much lower to the ground, and its 25 granite boulders remain intact in an unusually complex and intriguing double-circle formation. »

One of the megaliths

The moor hosts 11 separate sites

The puzzling hill

Above: Old stone sign for Electric Brae

Left: Machrie's central circle

The circles were used by Neolithic and Bronze Age farmers for religious and ceremonial purposes, with evidence of burials at each site, probably of elite members of the primitive societies.

Folklore says that one circle was named after a mythical giant named Fingal, who once tied his dog up to the stone while he ran an errand.

Keen-eyed visitors have also noticed that the stone circles align with a notch between hills on the horizon, through which the sun rises at the very peak of midsummer.

Could these magnificent standing stones be the magnetic force behind Electric Brae?

"Stone circles were created by fairies flicking pebbles"

If you believe local legend, the beauty spot is magical, with some stories stating that the stone circles were created by fairies flicking pebbles onto the moor from the top of a nearby hill.

Over the years, the sloped brae in Ayrshire has appeared in countless articles and TV programmes, and has attracted a huge number of tourists to the area, who are keen to try out the amazing road for themselves.

In fact, the stretch of road is so popular, that the area displays a sign warning that there will be slow-moving vehicles up ahead as drivers marvel at the effects.

Confused passengers, trying to get to grips with this incredible but eerie spectacle, can be spotted on a daily basis leaning out of vehicles to get a closer look.

Electric Brae, begins after a curve in the road of the A719 and features a slope of 1:86 upwards. The landscape on either side, however, creates an optical illusion, making it look as if the road is inclining the opposite way, and giving motorists the feeling that their cars are somehow freewheeling uphill.

Or perhaps the locals were right and the mystical car-pulling force actually originates from the standing stones across the water on the Isle of Arran. O

Words: DAWN GEDDES

THE MAIDEN STONE

Bride-to-be lost her life in bannock baking challenge with the devil

MOST brides-to-be leave the cooking to someone else on their wedding day, but the daughter of the laird of Balquhain decided to don her pinny and whip up some bannocks for her guests.

According to an Aberdeenshire legend, a stranger appeared and bet her that he could build a road to the top of Bennachie – a range of hills two miles away from her kitchen – faster than she could make another batch of bannocks.

Since construction usually takes a lot longer than cooking, she accepted the challenge.

No sooner had the laird's daughter got to work on the last of her bannocks than the road was miraculously completed. It turned out that the man was the devil himself. She ran for her life.

As God turned her into stone to protect her, the devil grabbed her shoulder – and that's why the Maiden Stone near Inverurie has its distinctive notch.

The stone itself is much older than the tale, and is one of the finest examples of Pictish carving in north-east Scotland, and is well worth seeking out. Just don't accept any baking challenges while you're there. O

The Maiden Stone

Bannocks

Mither Tap, Bennachie

"It turned out that the man was the devil"

Words: LAURA BROWN

"Circle builders used the mountain peaks as reference points"

Part of the Ring of Brodgar

STANDING THE TEST OF TIME

Stunning stone circles inspired and mystified for centuries

HUNDREDS of stone circles have been discovered in Scotland, but why were they built? The short answer is that no one knows for sure. Theories include places of worship, sacrifice, burial, a season indicator, astronomical observatory, an alarm clock, or simply a meeting point.

One theory even claims they were traps to imprison large animals – although this has mostly been debunked.

Most of the circles have been found to align with certain star systems but to what end?

We may never know the purpose of the circles, but that purpose must have been incredibly important to the ancient peoples who built them.

Creating a stone circle would have been a huge undertaking – across generations. Giant slabs of rock, each weighing tonnes, had to be cut and transported miles to the chosen site.

Then there was the business of hauling these stones upright, digging the surrounding ditch, and calculating the exact measurements to get a perfect circle.

Ancient stone circles are not just native to Scotland, or indeed the UK – they can be found throughout Europe, often in mountainous landscapes. Many were uncovered in the Pyrenees between Spain and France, in the Cévennes in southern France, in the Alps, and in Bulgaria.

Most date from around 3000BCE, but some are as much as 2000 years older than that. It is thought the circle builders used the peaks of the mountains as ➤➤

Calanais Standing Stones

reference points for aligning the stones. The exact number of stone circles in Scotland is not clear, but they are found all over the country, and sometimes in the most unlikely of places.

One of the most instantly-recognisable circles, is at Callanish on the Isle of Lewis in the Outer Hebrides. The stones here are thought to have been erected even earlier than Stonehenge, between 2900 and 2600BCE, with evidence of even earlier structures .

Also called Calanais in Scottish Gaelic, the Callanish complex extends out much farther than its central stone circle. Centred around the main circle, Callanish One,

"It would've taken 50 workers a year"

lie dozens of other formations, including three other circles and several arcs and single stones all overlooking Loch Roag.

Callanish One rests in almost a Celtic cross-shaped formation that runs for well over 100 metres (328 feet), north to south.

The circle, made of 13 stones spaced out to give a space of 11.4m (37.4ft) in diameter, is at the centre of the cross. Scientists estimate it would have taken 50 workers a whole year to transport and erect each stone to their place.

Interestingly, the four arms of the cross point almost directly to the compass points north, east, south and west. The flat sides of the central stone, at 4.8m (16ft) tall, also face north and south.

This uniformity suggests the stones were erected to aid observation of the night skies, although according to one story, the stones were giants who would not convert to Christianity and were petrified.

Orion's Belt

Stones of Stenness

Ring of Brodgar

It has also been said that Callanish had some link to Clisham mountain further south on the Isle of Harris.

The stones all come from the same source of Lewisian gneiss – the oldest rock in the UK, giving them an air of mystical intrigue.

A small chambered tomb was discovered within the central circle of Callanish. Pottery fragments were found here, as well as beaker vessels, which date to around 2000 – 1700BCE, indicating the tomb was in use for centuries after its construction.

The Ring of Brodgar on Orkney, is another fascinating stone circle, and the largest in Scotland. It dates back to 3000BCE, and was originally comprised of 60 stones.

The stones themselves are red sandstone and reach between two metres (seven feet) and a whopping 4.5m (15ft) tall. Today, 27 are still standing in their original positions – in a true circle, 103m (340ft) in diameter.

Some say the circle was used to chart the rise of the moon and constellations to tell the passage of the seasons. As more of the structure was unearthed, it became clear that the stone circle was part of a much larger prehistoric complex.

To the south east of the Ring of Brodgar stands another stone circle, the Stones of Stenness. Four giant megaliths, at 4.8m (16ft) , date to 3100BCE making it one of the oldest circles in the UK.

In the centre is a large stone hearth made of four large stone slabs, where cremated bone, charcoal and pottery were found. The entrance to the stone circle faces the nearby Barnhouse settlement, an excavated group of house dwellings dating from around 3000BCE.

A map of the Ring of Brodgar, shows the Stones of Stenness and the Stones of Bookan to the north west, in a mirror image of Orion's Belt in the night sky. O

Words: SAM LEWIS

CRATHES CALENDAR

The oldest lunar time tracker built by hunter-gatherers

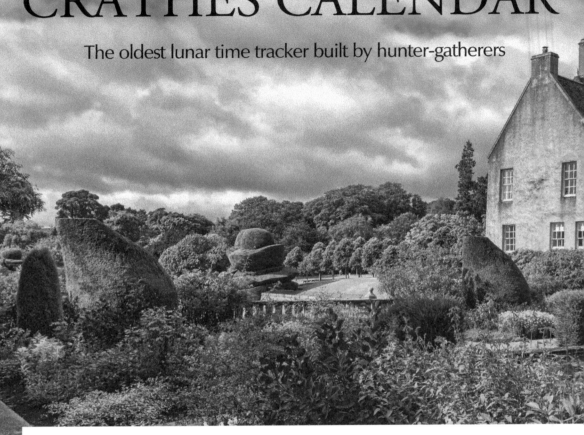

I N 2004, archaeologists found what they believe to be the world's oldest calendar – in a neglected field on the estate of Crathes Castle in Aberdeenshire.

An aerial survey by the Royal Commission on the Ancient and Historical Monuments of Scotland (RCAHMS) happened to discover unusual crop marks in the grounds and alerted the archaeology department at the University of Birmingham.

A team was deployed to investigate, and their excavations with the National Trust for Scotland between 2004 and 2006 uncovered a series of 12 pits, appearing to mimic the phases of the moon to track the lunar months. One of the pits also appeared to align with sunrise on the midwinter solstice.

The people that created them around 8000BCE would have been hunter-gatherers, who relied on the food resources available in the local area for sustenance.

It is believed that creating the pits enabling them to track the seasons – important for recording when certain migrating animals would be around to hunt or when different berries would be ripe.

Wild berries

Crathes Castle

Sun at winter solstice

A modern lunar calendar

MOON CALENDAR

"It is believed to be the first constructed monument to track time"

The ancient calendar is believed to have been created around 10,000 years ago – making it the oldest known lunar calendar in the world.

The site is nearly 5000 years older than the first formal calendars previously found in Mesopotamia, which is western Asia today. Warren Field, as the site has been named, is therefore believed to be the first constructed monument to track time.

The site has provided an important glimpse into the lives and culture of hunter-gatherers and their relationship with the night sky as most monument building is associated with sedentary farmers. O

Words: KATRINA PATRICK

SYMBOLIC CIRCLES

This repeating prehistoric pattern is found throughout the world

STRANGE cup-and-ring markings adorn many of Scotland's ancient monuments. These distinctive and significant shapes form a kind of prehistoric art carved into rocks, especially Neolithic stone circles and monoliths.

They can be found throughout most coastal countries in Europe and similar symbols have been unearthed in Australia and India. The universality and similarity of the art is perplexing to anthropologists and archaeologists today.

A typical cup-and-ring mark consists of a smooth round impression into a rockface, like a small cup, surrounded by concentric circles moving out from the cup, like ripples. Much like the megalithic monuments they so often adorn, there are many theories as to the purpose of the cup and ring marks.

One suggestion is that prehistoric peoples were documenting important constellations in the night sky, or trying to understand orbits. Alternatively, their frequent appearance at burial cairns and other megalithic sites may imply a ritualistic or religious purpose.

Others claim that the carvings may have acted as a warning, marking out a group's territory to others, or simply been a way to decorate important places. O

Marks on standing stones

"The carvings perplex archaeologists"

CRAMOND LIONESS

Stunning Roman relic found preserved in River Almond mud

O NE day in 1997, ferryman Robert Graham spotted a stone ear and eye sticking out of mud on the banks of the River Almond at Cramond, Edinburgh, but it proved too heavy to unearth.

By chance, an archaeologist climbed aboard his boat a few months later to cross the river and Robert asked her to have a look at what he'd found.

Excitement ensued – it turned out the sculpture was very special indeed. Experts from the local council's archaeology service were called, and confirmed that the lioness sculpture was a Roman relic.

Cramond was the site of a Roman fort and, although many relics have been found over the years, this was the most important artefact to be uncovered here.

The Cramond Lioness is believed to have watched over the tomb of a Roman dignitary. She's five feet long and in remarkable condition considering her 1800 years spent in the silt. After a lengthy period of drying out, she went on display in the National

The Cramond Lioness

Museum of Scotland, where she can still be seen today.

For his part in preserving this magnificent piece of history, Robert received a £50,000 finder's fee – though he admitted he would have preferred to keep the statue. O

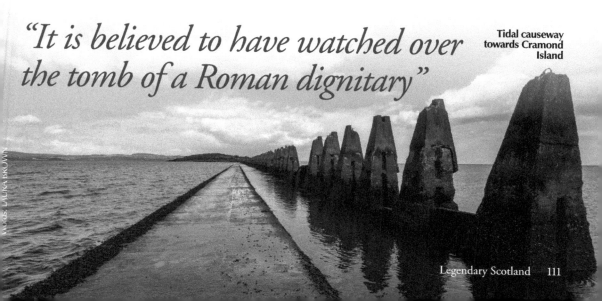

"It is believed to have watched over the tomb of a Roman dignitary"

Tidal causeway towards Cramond Island

WORDS: LAURA BROWN

TOP ANCIENT SITES

Get hands-on with history at these amazingly well-preserved brochs, cairns and fortifications peppered throughout Scotland

1 Cairnpapple Hill, West Lothian

Cairnpapple Hill lies in the middle of the Central Belt, not far from places where micro-electronics and high finance are the daily norm. Tucked away in the Bathgate Hills is a burial chamber with a history dating back more than 4000 years – you can clamber inside with the use of a ladder and experience the stillness of this ancient tomb. Outside, look out over the hills, across the Firth of Forth and south to the Southern Uplands. Even superbly preserved prehistoric sites like this never suffer from over-crowding, so it's perfect for a picnic, too.

2

Edin's Hall Broch, Abbey St Bathans, Borders

The double ramparts of Edin's Hall Broch, sitting on top of a hill high above the Whiteadder Water are impressive, especially when you consider they date back up to 2500 years ago. A walk up to the Iron Age hillfort from the village of Abbey St Bathans will test the leg muscles for just under an hour and emphasise the ingenuity of our ancestors. This broch is a rare example in the Lowlands and its large size means that whoever had it built was a person of power. Today, it's a good place to explore and stop for a snack.

3 Rough Castle, Near Falkirk

This is almost modern compared to others here, but still ancient. Construction began on the Antonine Wall around 142CE, and it stretches from Bo'ness on the River Forth to Old Kilpatrick on the Clyde. Much of it consisted of a large ditch with fortifications such as Rough Castle. It was the north-west frontier of the Roman Empire until it was abandoned around 160CE, and is still impressive. Look for pits which held stakes designed to impale would-be invaders. They were called "lilia" as Caesar thought they looked like lilies.

4 Jarlshof, Sumburgh, Shetland

Jarlshof was in use by humans for more than 4000 years. Up until the 1600s it was a place of homes, farming and ritual. A partially-ruined Iron Age broch sits near a Bronze Age smithy, as well as a Norse longhouse. This is a complex site and a 16th-century laird's house is also there to be explored, dominating the surrounding landscape. When you add in the dramatic headland on which it all lies, this makes for an exciting place to experience. It was Sir Walter Scott who named the site Jarlshof, or "earl's house", in his novel *The Pirate*. Its proper name is Sumburgh.

5 Clachtoll Broch, Sutherland

White sands, turquoise waters and mountain views make Clachtoll Beach one of Scotland's most beautiful coastal spots, but when you add an Iron Age structure dating back more than 2000 years you will definitely want to stay a while. Not far from the beach is a huge pile of stones which, on closer inspection, become the easily identifiable remains of an Iron Age broch – the entrance to which you can crawl into. Although the roof has collapsed it is still amazing to be able to go through the old doorway after two millennia.

6 Cairn o'Get, Caithness

Caithness is one of the best places in Scotland to visit prehistoric sites – there are so many that they appear round almost every corner – and this burial chamber is one of the best. The chamber dates back more than 5000 years, and you can walk through the entrance and be transported back to the time of early man, when family burials were a cornerstone of the culture. Although the roof is missing, the workmanship is still there to be admired – as well as the peace and tranquillity of this unspoiled corner of Scotland.

Words: NICK DRAINEY

Legendary Scotland Books

A-Z Of Great Scots

The award-winning team behind The Scots Magazine brings you an A – Z of some of the great unsung Scottish heroes from throughout history. From Agnes Randolph, who single-handedly defended a castle against an army of 20,000 in the 14th century to William Kidd the privateer and inspiration behind Treasure Island. Plus, discover Andrew Watson, the first black person to play professional and international football, and Isabel Newstead MBE, who won nine Paralympic medals in swimming, shooting and athletics. This book celebrates the diversity and canniness of Scotland's people – in all fields, and from all walks of life. 116-page paperback.

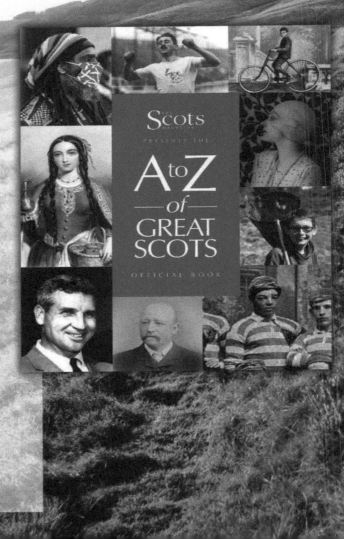

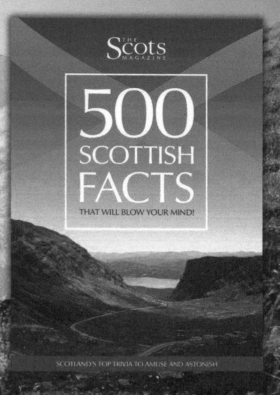

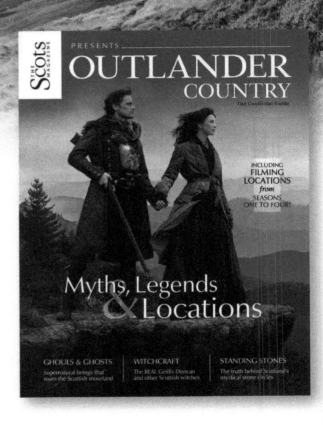